THE

SABBATH-SCHOOL

INDEX.

POINTING OUT

THE HISTORY AND PROGRESS OF SUNDAY-SCHOOLS, WITH APPROVED MODES OF INSTRUCTION, EXAMPLES IN ILLUSTRATIVE, PICTORIAL, AND OBJECT-TEACHING; ALSO THE USE OF THE BLACKBOARD, MANAGEMENT OF INFANT-CLASSES, TEACHERS' MEETINGS, CONVENTIONS, INSTITUTES, ETC., ETC., ETC.

BY R. G. PARDEE, A. M.

PHILADELPHIA:
J. C. GARRIGUES & CO.,
148 SOUTH FOURTH STREET,
1868.

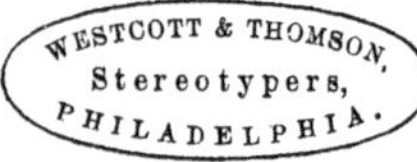

Jas. B. Rodgers, Pr.
52 & 54 N. 6th St.

PREFACE.

A FEW years ago the author prepared a little Manual entitled "The Sunday-School Worker Assisted," etc., which was so favorably received as to call for a large edition without any special advertising. What has seemed to be a most imperative call has again come up, from various sections of our land, and from many denominations of Christians, for a fuller and more complete work, illustrated with examples. If our pastors, superintendents or teachers, wished for specific details of all the departments of the Sabbath-school, they complained that they were compelled to purchase a dozen English and a dozen American works, and even then there were important topics of information still unreached. Besides, books written a quarter of a century ago will not fully meet the requirements of an intelligent Sabbath-school man at this day. The cause is making constant progress, and many real improvements have been made during the past few years which are worthy of special record and notice.

Never before has the Holy Bible been so exalted, so taught, so applied, and made so interesting as now. Never before were our best Sabbath-schools devoted to such pure, simple, child-like worship of God as now; and never before was the high and holy aim of *immediate conversion* of the scholars to Christ, and then their thorough religious training, kept steadily in view, as it is in many Sunday-schools at the present time.

The Sabbath-school, as the true working-field of the Christian churches ("The Bible School," as Dr. Chalmers called it), is now the grand rallying cry of the faithful.

The aim and design of this work is to observe, collate, and condense, as far as possible, the *best* thoughts, experience, and observation of Sabbath-school laborers and authors, not only in this country but also in Great Britain, and to combine these with the observation and experience of the writer during the last forty-five years. The author is greatly indebted particularly to the London Sunday-School Union publications, and to *The Sunday-School Times* of Philadelphia, as well as to most of his fellow-laborers and writers in both countries. Gladly would he give credit in every instance, but their works have been so read and their thoughts gathered up, preserved, and noted for use during many years, and their views so assimilated with the author's and made his own, that he is now quite unable to trace them accurately to their right sources. They have become the property of all, and he has appropriated and adopted them into the line of his own thought in the one great work.

The best examples and the best new improvements are here given for the Sabbath-school artist to copy. No one man or school or country embodies them all. None, however, are mere theories. Everything here stated has been tried and proved.

The future progress of the Sabbath-school will be carefully watched, in order to add to or modify subsequent editions of this book, so that the Sabbath-school worker, with no other guide-board but this "Index," may be enabled, by divine grace, to enter the right path and to do a good Christian work in training up the children and youth of his generation.

THE AUTHOR.

NEW YORK, *February*, 1868.

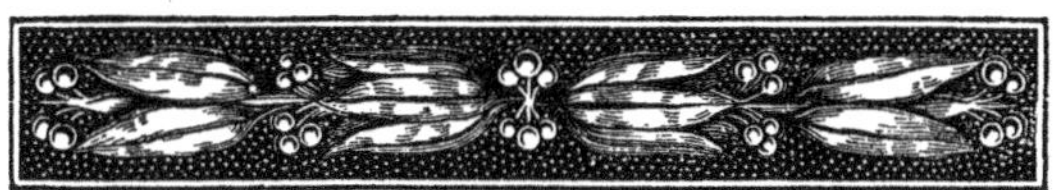

CONTENTS.

THE

SABBATH-SCHOOL INDEX.

I.

THE SABBATH-SCHOOL.

T is a place where the churches of Christ meet with the children and youth for the worship and service of God. It is the Church of God caring for the children on the Sabbath day. Every song of praise, as well as every prayer and reading and study of the Word of God, together with every exhortation, address or sermon, should rise to a high and holy act of simple, life-like, child-like devotion. The place should be comfortable, attractive, light, airy and cheerful. It should be dry and well warmed. The walls may be covered with prints, hymns, and Scripture mottoes; or, as some of our wealthy congregations have done, they may be frescoed beautifully with illuminated texts or

paintings representing Scripture scenes, to attract the children to the house of God—to their *Sabbath Home*. Especial care should be taken that the seats provided are adapted in size, height, and form, to all ages and sizes, from the wee ones in the infant classes up to the larger scholars and the members of the adult classes. The three-sides-of-an-octagon form of seat is found to answer well, and is much cheaper than the circular seats. Infant classes will need a room by themselves, and sometimes raised seats are to be preferred. A good blackboard and crayons, with good maps, should be furnished to every room, together with a well-selected library, both for teachers and scholars. Keep on file a few good Sunday-school papers and magazines. It would be well also to have a few reference Bibles and a Bible Dictionary. But the glory of the Sabbath-school is the open Bible, the living Teacher, the Church Militant and aggressive. Said De Witt Clinton: "The Sunday-school is one of the three great powers by which the moral world is to be moved." Says the Rev. Dr. Daggett: "The Sabbath-school is to do vastly more than all other agencies of the Church." Said John Angell James: "In a few years we shall look upon all the past progress of the Sunday-school but as the beginning, as a kind of first-fruits, an earnest of the future of this great institution of the Christian Church." Said the Rev. Dr. Campbell, of the *British Banner*, London: "With respect to countless multitudes, it is mainly the work of the Sunday-school teacher to carry out the command of our Lord to preach the gospel to every creature. The Sunday-school, for the *individual*, for the *family*, for the *Church*, for the *nation*, and for the *world*, is one of the principal mottoes to be inscribed on the banners of the faithful; and many well-meant but feeble agencies on which much religious activity is now *frittered* away, will, we believe, at length be merged in this grand institution. The conviction is strong in our mind that the Sunday-school Union, as a great central source of light, life, and power, is on the threshhold of a glorious career of usefulness, and will speedily become, in the hands of the great Master, an agency for good to an extent beyond all present appreciation by the Christian Church."

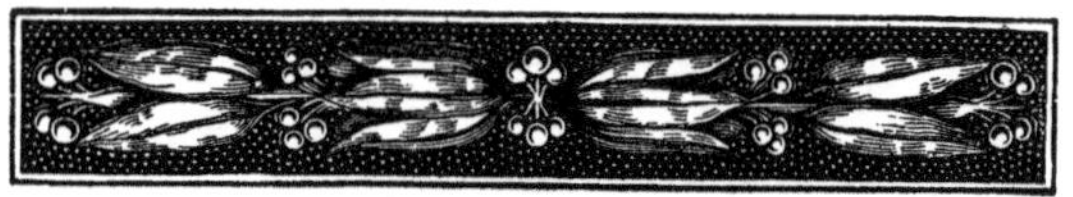

II.

HISTORY AND PROGRESS.

HE history of Sabbath-schools is nearly allied to the onward progress of the Church of God in the earth. In all ages, whenever pure religion has been revived, it would seem that especial attention has always been given to the early religious instruction and training of children and youth by the Church of God; and herein lies the grand SUNDAY-SCHOOL IDEA. Says a Scotch divine: "Vital religion, and the godly upbringing of the young, have ever gone hand in hand." The soul is diseased, and a Bible education is the only remedy. In that wonderful BOOK, which extends its record over the long period of four thousand years of this world's history, there is throughout a wonderful regard for children. Of the patriarch Abraham, nearly four thousand years ago, it is written: "For I know him, that he will command his children and his household after him, and they shall keep the way of the Lord." Gen. xviii. 19. With what wonderful power does the history of the childhood of Joseph, and Moses, and David, and Samuel, and Daniel, illus-

trate the value of the instruction and religious training of children.

When Moses, the great lawgiver of Israel, received the law amid the thunderings and lightnings and earthquakes of Mount Sinai, he called "All Israel" together (Deut. v. 1), and by divine direction his words were (Deut. vi. 6): "Hear, O *Israel*, ... These words, which I command thee this day, shall be (1) in thine heart: and (2) thou shalt *teach* them diligently unto thy children," etc., *i. e.*, the *Church's* children—not parents exclusive, but inclusive of course. "Israel," that was called upon by Moses, was the Church of God upon earth, and it is her express duty to the end of time to see that all her children shall be "taught of the Lord." It is true that parents are the divinely-appointed guardians and instructors of their children, and this obligation rests upon them; and yet they are, alas! too often incapable of the religious instruction of their own children or of any other, besides being often indifferent; and the Church of God, by her catechetical or Sabbath-school instruction, has always had, and probably will always have, to supply the lack of unfaithful parents. There is no agency which so supplies the lack of *mothers* as a good Sabbath-school.

Thus we find in Deuteronomy, nearly four thousand years ago, the great Sabbath-school principle foreshadowed and embodied; and where, we may ask, can be found in all the Bible a more definite authorization or *divine appointment* for any of the great denominational Christian Churches which now so bless our land than is here found for the Sabbath-school? It is ordained and blessed of God. The Sabbath-school is simply the Church of Christ putting forth its legitimate effort in its most inviting field of action. It is *the* regular systematic working department of the Christian Church—not an outside auxiliary, but an inside,—the Church itself in action; and as such let it be carefully guarded and cherished. The same Divine lips which said "Go preach," said also and equally to his disciples, "Go *teach*." Says the Rev. J. H. Vincent: "There is just as much divine authority for the Sabbath-school as there is for the sanctuary—no more." Our Divine Lord and Master himself repeatedly astonished his own disciples by his particular notice of and care for little children, and with sore displeasure he rebuked his followers for hindering them from being brought to him.

It was not until nearly the close of the second century, or, according to Tertullian, in the year A. D. 180, that the Christian Church felt compelled, in order to check the defection of heathen converts, to set about the establishment of those celebrated catechumenical schools, of which Origen was one of the catechists, for the systematic religious instruction by the Church of Christ of the children and youth.

So useful and necessary, however, did this work prove itself to be, that very soon similar schools were universally established. They continued to flourish until near the close of the sixth century, when they declined and became obscured for ten long centuries in the gloom of the Dark Ages, with only an occasional prince, or pastor, or layman in the spirit of the Master, to teach the children the way of life.

In the sixteenth century, however, on the dawn of the Reformation, Martin Luther established his celebrated Sunday-schools at Wittemberg in the year 1527; and soon after John Knox inaugurated the Sunday-schools of Scotland, "with readers," as the history of Scotland informs us, in 1560; so that on the incoming of the Reformation the children were again "taught of the Lord." In the year 1580, Borromeo, the pious Archbishop of Milan, established a system of Sunday-schools throughout his large diocese in Lombardy.

In our own land our Pilgrim Fathers early entered upon the work; for Ellis, in his History of Roxbury, Massachusetts, says: "In 1674, 6th 11th month, is the first record of a Sabbath-school." The records of the Pilgrim Church in Plymouth, Massachusetts, inform us that a Sabbath-school was there organized as early as in 1680. Joseph Alleine, the author of the "Alarm to the Unconverted," opened a Sabbath-school in England in 1688, and many others might be mentioned in both countries in succession. But the first Sabbath-school of which we have any *authentic, definite, and detailed* account, extending over a period of a quarter of a century, was that established by Ludwig Hacker in Ephratah, Lancaster county, Pennsylvania, as early as the year 1747. It was continued uninterruptedly during a period of more than thirty years, until the building was taken for a soldiers' hospital in the time of the Revolutionary War. It enjoyed precious seasons of revival, and had its children's meetings, and we are informed that many children were hopefully converted to God. We have before us a long letter from Dr. Fahnestock to the Rev. W. T. Brantley, D. D., of Philadelphia, written in 1835, detailing many interesting facts connected with the history of this Sabbath-school, drawn from living pupils and records.

Robert Raikes instituted not only, but *organized*, the SYSTEM of Sabbath-schools, and popularized them in England, in Gloucester, in February, 1781. All benevolence was single-handed until such men as Robert Raikes and William Wilberforce *organized* it, and sent it forth systematized on its errand of love, mercy and salvation throughout the world. Before this, as we have seen, there were isolated occasional Sabbath-schools, but their influence was confined mainly to one city, one town, or one church, and expired with an individual. But Robert Raikes "founded Sabbath-schools for the Church universal." John Wesley preached and *organized*. George Whitefield preached, and did not organize. Robert Raikes *organized* Sabbath-schools, but his predecessors did not do so. And we can in both cases see the important difference. Within the short space of four years from the period when Mr. Raikes established his first Sabbath-school in Gloucester, England, more than one-quarter of a million of children in England were enjoying the blessing of Sabbath-school instruction. All honor, then, to Robert Raikes!

To Bishop Ashbury appears to belong the honor of first introducing Robert Raikes's idea of Sabbath-schools into this country, in Virginia in 1786. How long the school was continued, or what was its influence in Virginia, we are unable to state.

The first "Sunday-school *Society*" was formed in London, September 7, 1785. This was on the system of paid teachers, but when the plan of voluntary, unpaid teachers had become established, this society gave place to the present "London Sunday-School Union," which was organized to meet this change on the 13th of July, 1803. Both of these societies were formed on the union plan, including the various denominations, the first including an equal number of Churchmen and Dissenters in its management.

The First-day or Sunday-School Society in Philadelphia was organized in 1791, and Bishop White was its first president.

We learn from a carefully prepared editorial in the first volume of the "Sunday-School Teacher's Magazine and Journal of Education," published in New York, 1823, that after a careful personal interview of the editor with the parties, he had been enabled to ascertain the precise time and the circumstances under which the first Sabbath-school was commenced in New York city. Mr. and Mrs.

Divie Bethune had spent part of the years 1801 and 1802 in England, where they had observed the progress of Sunday-schools in Great Britain; and on their return, in connection with their pious mother, the late Mrs. Isabella Graham, they arranged their plans, and "in the autumn of 1803 these three Christian philanthropists opened the first Sunday-school in New York for religious and catechetical purposes, at their own expense, at the house of Mrs. Leech, in Mott street." Mrs. Graham and Mr. and Mrs. Bethune then established two other Sabbath-schools in other parts of the city, and soon after one for the children in the alms-house in New York. It is to the same source, too, that *adult* schools owe their commencement in this country, or at least in New York. Mrs. Graham, it is stated, opened the first adult school in Greenwich, in 1814, on the second Sabbath in June, only about two months before her death. We are thus particular to state these facts, for we are aware that a later date has been insisted upon for the inauguration of the first Sunday-school of New York.

Samuel Slater opened a school for his operatives in Pawtucket, Rhode Island, in 1797. The Broadway Baptist Sabbath-school, in Baltimore, was established in 1804, and it is said to be still in operation. Mrs. Amos Tappan (Miss Buckminster) opened a Sabbath-school in Portsmouth, New Hampshire, in 1803. We do not learn that the Churches and organized Christian bodies took hold of the Sabbath-school movement in this country, so as to *produce* permanent and efficient *action*, until 1809, when we find an elaborate constitution and plan of action from Pittsburgh, Pennsylvania. In 1810 a Sabbath-school was organized in Beverly, Massachusetts, and in Boston in 1812. Soon after this there began to be a more general and awakened interest in the Churches in behalf of Sabbath-schools, and the years 1814, 1815, and 1816 were years of most triumphant progress, so that in 1817 Sunday-schools were organized in most of our flourishing churches and Christian communities throughout this country.

Early in 1816 the New York Sunday-School Union was established, and is the first and oldest Union in our land, having just celebrated its semi-centennial. The American Sunday-School Union was organized in 1824, to provide a juvenile Christian literature (and from whence our public school district libraries borrowed their first idea) and to plant a Sunday-school wherever there is a population.

Surely, if any work in our land needs to be hastened, it is that of the religious instruction of the neglected children and youth of this nation by means of Sabbath-schools. Not to mention the various modern denominational movements, the above we believe to be a correct history of the Sunday-school progress, and we suppose it to be sufficiently full for practical purposes in this work. We have ample materials on this subject to fill a large volume, but this may here suffice.

There are other questions, however, which ought to be here recorded in connection with the progress of the cause. In Great Britain the work is embarrassed from the fact that as a general rule only the children of the poor and middle classes attend their Sabbath-schools. In the early stages of the Sabbath-school movement in this country the same custom prevailed here, and it is certainly worthy of record by what means the change was effected.

Several years ago, while in attendance upon a Sunday-school meeting, the writer of this enjoyed a lengthened interview with the late Rev. Dr. Lyman Beecher, then in his prime. Our conversation turned upon that unfortunate feature of the cause in England which virtually excluded all the better-to-do children of that country. Dr. Beecher's eye lit up at once, and with great animation, as he said to me: "It was the same here at first, and I do not know but I had an important hand in producing the change. I saw the tendency of things, and feared that our Sunday-schools would result in a failure if only the poor children gained the benefit of them in this land, and it troubled me for some year or two. At last," said he, energetically, "I resolved to overthrow that system, and went and called upon Judge W., one of my most influential families, and said, 'Judge W——, I want you to bring your children to Sunday-school next Sabbath.' '*Me!*' exclaimed the Judge in amazement. 'Yes, you,' calmly responded Dr. Beecher: 'I have made up my mind to take *my children*, and I want you and a few others of the best families to popularize the thing.' A little explanation secured the object. He then called upon Mrs. S——, the most aristocratic lady in the community, and said, 'Mrs. S—— I want you to lead *your two daughters* into our Sunday-school next Sabbath;' and, said the Doctor, 'Mrs. S—— almost shouted in astonishment;' but a more particular and careful explanation than sufficed with Judge W—— succeeded here; and then the family of the first physician was in like manner secured, and we all turned our labor and influence on the Sunday-school movement, and it gave an unheard-of impetus to our Sunday-school, and by means of the press and by letters and personal conversation the facts became known and met with almost universal approval and adoption in our country, and the reform soon became complete." Blessings, a thousand blessings rest upon the memory of the man, or the men and women, who aided to bring about this glorious change in this land!

The law of progress is very noticeable in the teaching of the Sabbath-school. Robert Raikes's first idea was scarcely more than to keep the children out of the streets and to protect the Sabbath. Then the children were taught to read and write. After that a great advance was made by the introduction of the Bible as the reading-book; the next step was to commit the Bible to memory; and then the Christian Churches took hold of the Sabbath-school.

For awhile *Memory* was crowded to its utmost extent, to the injury of the scholar, and mere memorizing became the hobby in most of our schools. After a while the physicians checked this, by telling us that by crowding the memory we were developing a new disease amongst children, viz., Hydrocephalus, or water on the brain. Then our schools were in trouble, and resort was had to question-cards, and finally question-books became the hobby. In a few years question-books began to be stale and monotonous, and we appealed to the imagination and resorted to stories and anecdotes until they wearied, and then we searched commentaries, and theology was administered to the children in large doses. After that what was called spiritual teaching was adopted, but that soon degenerated into mere exhortation. Now we find that we must comprehensively grasp and rightly use them all, and make a hobby of none. The *memory* is the grand store-house of the mind, and it should be well filled; but it is folly to overstock it and overwhelm the brain. The *imagination* is God's grand medium of worship and communion with him and the spiritual world. We cannot worship God without it. Let us not exorcise it because some abuse it. "The *imagination* has the same place in the faculties that the eye has among the senses." The *intellect* is God's great gift which distinguishes man from the brute. Let us never worship nor pervert it. The *heart* is the soul of man. To save it the Son of man came down from heaven to earth. Unless the heart is gained all is lost; but if we appeal to the heart alone, we but develop the puny Christian. Let us, therefore, use all wisely, but misuse none. At first the aim of Sabbath-school teaching was very feeble and indefinite: to keep the children out of mischief—teach them to read the Bible —correct their manners and make them good children —not profane and disobedient. Then the aim was to give them a general knowledge of Bible history and catechism. The ablest early Sabbath-school works published under the patronage of the Queen of England did not even hint at the possible conversion of the children. The Bible was long introduced as a book of task lessons to the young, and catechism and hymn learning engrossed our Bible classes. Now, the Bible is exalted, and so applied in our Sabbath-schools as to be the most attractive of all books to the children and youth. Now, the aim of Sabbath-school teaching is, or ought to be, the *immediate* conversion of the children to Christ. It is a poor excuse to suffer a child to drown because we have but one opportunity of saving it. *Now*, many Sabbath-school teachers have learned the great and precious art of leading even little children to Jesus—"Just now."

Sabbath-schools are, as we believe, about to enter upon a great and glorious career, compared with which all the past history of the cause is but as the early dawn before a bright and glorious day; and this era is the culture and training by the word and grace of God of all that constitutes the best style of man and Christian; for we hold it to be the true teacher's position that there is no weakness or infirmity of temper, habit, purpose, or character in any of our pupils that the Sabbath-school, with its divine text-book and the promised Spirit of God, is not perfectly competent to remove. Let this be our standard, and according to our faith be it unto us. May the great Master so bless and prosper this heaven-born institution that speedily "our children may *all* be taught of the Lord, and that great may be the peace of our children."

III.

CONVENTIONS.

THE object of these gatherings is to arouse, to instruct, and to train. 1. To explore the districts, report the destitutions, and devise the best ways of filling up existing schools, of planting new schools, and reaching, if possible, every neglected child. 2. To call attention to the bad or inefficient habits in the modes of conducting and teaching in our Sabbath-schools, and to suggest a remedy by detailing the more excellent ways. 3. To instruct and train teachers how they may prepare and teach the lesson better, and how they can become better acquainted with children's character, language, and feelings. It is of prime importance that there should be frequent and earnest conferences of pastors, superintendents, and teachers, in order to become acquainted with all the best modes and real improvements that the most favored enjoy. A quarter of a century or more ago, county Sunday-school conventions and anniversaries were frequently held, but they were usually crowded into a single afternoon, giving the Bible Society the morning and the

Temperance Union the evening of the day. The time was insufficient to examine the state of the cause, or the schools, with much care, although the meetings were uniformly pleasant, and sometimes of considerable interest; yet their influence was quite limited and evanescent.

It was during the early autumn of 1856 that the good Spirit prompted the Sabbath-school teachers of Massachusetts, one thousand strong, to pay a visit to the Crystal Palace and the Sabbath-school teachers of New York. They were received with great cordiality, and mingled delightfully with the Sabbath-school teachers of New York and Brooklyn during two or three days, closing with a grand Farewell Meeting in Plymouth Church, Brooklyn. This religious festival afforded a good opportunity for the Sabbath-school laborers from the various sections of the country to compare views and converse freely about all departments of the good work. All this proved to be interesting and profitable beyond all expectation, and the result was, there arose a very general desire to renew these prolonged conferences of teachers, under other forms, as soon as practicable.

Accordingly, Massachusetts called a three-days State Sabbath-school Convention, in the city of Boston, later in the fall of the same year; and New York held its first State Sabbath-school Convention, of three days, in the city of Albany, in the month of January, 1857. Both conventions were enthusiastic and useful, and those States have continued these meetings annually since that period; and most of the Northern States, and some of the Southern States, have followed the good example, with the most beneficial results. They have awakened much interest and aroused the people everywhere. Beside the State meetings, County and Town Sunday-school Conventions have been organized quite extensively, combining counsels and efforts in all directions. The States appointed County Secretaries or Vice-Presidents, and counties gave the same office to the towns, forming a medium of union and communication, exploration and effort throughout.

These conventions are very useful; but care must be taken or they will degenerate into dull, heavy routine, or wordy discussions, or tedious essays, or mere story-telling, or a waste of time in organizing.

The whole value of Sunday-school conventions depends, of course, upon the manner in which they are conducted. Like the teaching by a wrong mode, they can be made profoundly wearisome, when they should always be made profoundly interesting and profitable. Let the convention be called with GREAT CARE and EFFORT. Let the call always proceed from the right source. Consider well as to the right time and the right place. Then first carefully counsel with the leading pastors and superintendents of the various denominations, so that they may understand it and arrange for it. Get a pastor to speak particularly and personally beforehand to three or four of his most active, influential ladies, asking them to notify other families and arrange so as to favor the convention. Take the same course with the men; for we must have much personal effort in getting it up. Let the call state distinctly the object, and, as far as may be, the order of the meetings, and send it out as early as three or four weeks before the meeting, to all, and with particular care. Do not depend upon newspaper advertisements to give notice. Get as many pastors, superintendents, and teachers as possible to *pledge* a constant attendance at every meeting and be ready to aid at all times. Secure a light, cheerful, comfortable room. Place a large, clean black-board, with crayons and rubber, on the platform, together with a supply of paper and pencils for taking notes. Appoint a good leader of singing. Meet promptly, and commence the meeting punctually, although but few may be present. Let the first half-hour be one of warm, earnest devotion. Have some appropriate, burning words of Scripture —two or three verses—ready to kindle and glow in every heart. The prayers and hymns should all be brief and directly to the point of seeking the blessing of God, without which all the efforts will be vain. Without God we can do nothing. Next call to order naturally, and waste not a moment of time in a simple organization. Have an understanding beforehand and call a good, influential man, fitted to preside, to the chair, and appoint a suitable Secretary, and, perhaps, a Business Committee.

Then enter earnestly into the work before you. Wait not a moment for the business committee to report, but let the chairman call for reports from some section as to the state and prospects of Sabbath-schools. Gather information, and let that information be the *basis* of systematic action.

The missionary and aggressive feature should first claim attention. Care must be taken that unimportant routine of particular schools does not clog the convention. If in a State gathering, you can hardly have time to hear reports except from counties. If a county meeting, hear from towns; and if in a town gathering, you can descend and hear suggestive reports from schools, leading to right action. In other conventions, references to individual schools must be mostly in the way of some spirited illustration. Get a bird's-eye view of your whole field, and then detail the best plans of meeting deficiencies, so as to reach effectually the whole outlying population, either by voluntary effort, or by Sabbath-school missionaries, in filling up existing schools and planting others as needed. After a thorough canvass of your whole field, then inquire what are the great wants and difficulties in our present Sabbath-school operations? and how can we best remove them and introduce all the *real* modern improvements?

Descend next to details as to organization, good records, the library, superintendents, teachers, and how to get them and train them so as to be efficient; good order, music, prayers, and good teaching in the

Infant, Scripture, and Bible classes, with such helps as the black-board, object-lessons, map-drawing, Bible geography, and history; teachers' meetings, and how successfully and profitably to conduct them; missionary meetings, monthly concerts of prayer, temperance meetings, social gatherings, mothers' meetings in mission schools, and especially children's prayer-meetings; addresses, reviews, catechisms, &c., may all be considered.

Then again we want help for the teacher; how to teach, with examples of various modes; illustrative teaching, pictorial teaching; on the art of securing attention, and on the art of questioning; visiting, conversions, and training for Christian work and usefulness; how to enlist the Church, the parents, and the community, the pastors and church officers, in this great work. These and other subjects should be brought up, not for indefinite discussion and debate, but for careful information, deliberate thought, and suggestions resulting from observation and mature experience.

Let all things be so arranged that one topic will naturally flow into and call up another; and what you touch, handle well. If one subject is brought up, and no one is ready to take it up, pass on to another, until you come to one upon which some person has a question to raise, or a suggestion or information to offer, or an experience to refer to about it. Waste not a moment of time in pointless and prosy harangues. A good time merely, pleasant anecdotes, or touching recitals of dying children, or sharp discussions, are not sufficient to constitute a good Sabbath-school convention. The great idea of Sabbath-schools, be it never forgotten, is not singing, or exhibitions, or addresses, or concerts. It is to meet together for the saving worship of God, in the thoughtful study of his Holy Word, in the singing of his praise, and in solemn, believing prayer, through our Lord Jesus Christ. These are the high and holy objects to which all our conventions should contribute.

An important National Sabbath-school Convention was held in Philadelphia in the year 1859, and this gave an additional impulse to the cause. It was, however, during the years 1863 and 1864, that it was observed that these interesting Sabbath-school conventions were in danger of losing their power. They had fallen into a sort of routine, and had begun to be monotonous and stale to the regular attendants, because they were not sufficiently practical and profitable. The questions were, therefore, forced upon us, What must be done? What does the present crisis of the cause demand? How can our great gatherings be made more *useful?* Deliberation and counsel brought the answer: "We need more *instruction.*" Teachers need training. They need to be taught how to prepare the lesson; how to secure attention; how to teach infants, juveniles, and adults; how to apply Bible truths. Superintendents need instruction how to gain order; how to organize and classify; how to open, conduct, and address and review the school; how to train the teachers and enlist the interest and service of parents, pastors, and the churches. All need inspiring with the spirit that will go forth and plant new schools, and gather in and secure a good religious education to every child in the community. In the way of accomplishment of these grand results the obstacles were foreseen—such as prosy essays, tedious discussions, formal addresses or sermons, which generalized everything and rendered it nought. On the other hand, we found a surfeit of touching little stories and old anecdotes, and it became necessary to strike out boldly for a reformation and an entire change of base in our plan of operations. Accordingly resort was had to what are called Sunday-school Institutes.

IV.

INSTITUTES.

HEY have grown out of the idea of the Public-school Teachers' Institutes, which have been sustained for many years with interest and profit, the expenses being cheerfully met out of the State Treasury. Our Sabbath-school Institutes are modeled somewhat on the same plan. The object is, by means of practical essays, model lessons, lectures, and drill exercises, to train the teachers and officers for their work. Institutes differ from other conventions in calling out the audience in responses, recapitulations, and more detailed instruction. They will take their character very much from the character and course pursued by the conductor. No two persons, perhaps, would conduct them alike. For instance, one man would give more attention to superintending, addresses, public exercises, singing, etc. Another to the blackboard, object teaching, and sacred geography; while another still, would give more attention to methods of teaching, teachers' meetings, normal classes, model lessons, etc. We would prefer to combine ALL these things in their

due proportion, in every Institute, and make as complete and clear work on every point as possible. The great object is to make them *useful.* If this is secured, they will be all the more interesting. There are two great subjects which should always be before every Institute, as well as every convention, viz., 1. The extension of Sabbath-schools, so as to reach all of the neglected; 2. The elevation and improvement of existing schools; and they need improving, if not reforming, in every part.

The first idea of a Sabbath-school Institute that ever entered the mind of the writer was suggested to him by a pastor, Rev. W. A. Niles, in the State Sunday-school Convention at Buffalo, New York, in 1864. An experiment was soon successfully made, and since then they have become almost universally popular and useful. The same thought, we have since been informed, had been considered, and Institutes held by the Rev. J. H. Vincent, in the Western Methodist Conferences; and as long ago as 1827, the New York Sunday-school Union, in its Eleventh Annual Report, particularly recommended this plan "of a school for the training of Sabbath-school teachers."

The forms of these Institutes are various. Many are made up partly of convention and partly of Institute exercises. Ordinarily two or three days and evenings are entirely devoted to one, by a county, or district comprising a dozen counties. Another plan, when held in a city, is to devote all the evenings and a part of the afternoons of a week to it; as in New York city last year, and recently in Brooklyn; also, prefacing it with an elaborate sermon on the Sabbath evening previous. Another plan still is to devote the usual weekly Teachers' Meeting of a school to a regular normal class or training Institute. All these plans are useful in the hands of a good conductor.

The Subjects

for consideration in an Institute may be suggested as follows:

1. How to form new schools.
2. How best to gather in the children.
3. Their conversion and culture.
4. Organization and classification.
5. Superintendents' duties.
6. Opening and closing exercises.
7. The library and record books.
8. The Bible classes.
9. The intermediate classes.
10. The infant-school.
11. Anniversaries and concerts.
12. Reviews and catechisms.
13. Children's prayer-meetings.
14. Training of converts.
15. How to teach; with model lessons and examples of good modes.
16. Illustrative teaching.
17. Object teaching.
18. Pictorial teaching.

19. The use of the blackboard.
20. The art of questioning.
21. The art of securing attention.
22. The preparation of the lesson.
23. Teachers' meetings.
24. Sunday-school music.
25. Children's prayers and devotions.
26. Map drawing.
27. Bible geography, history, etc.
28. Temperance meetings.

The Exercises

of an Institute may be—

1. Devotional exercises for specific objects.

2. Reports of superintendents and teachers as to how they do it, or reports of the destitution, wants, or difficulties.

3. Instruction by the conductor to meet the above specific wants and difficulties.

4. Questions by teachers and answers by the conductor to meet the points in the subject not fully explained.

5. Preparation lessons, practice lessons, and model lessons.

6. Explanatory and instructive addresses, lectures or essays.

7. Model Opening Exercises and Teachers' Meetings.

6. Drill exercises on activity, curiosity, inquisi

tiveness; or how to gain attention, how to instruct, how to impress, etc.

Every one should take some part in an Institute, *i. e.*, take notes, ask or answer questions, or give information or lessons. Let none be mere spectators. Always have plenty of paper for taking notes, also pencils, and provide a good blackboard and crayons, and perhaps a map, together with a good warm, light and pleasant room to meet in.

Get up the Institute with care. Have it all well understood, and then talk about it, write and print about it, and get teachers and pastors pledged to attend. Pray much for the Institute, and select the best time, and do all that you undertake to do, thoroughly and well. Let one subject naturally glide into the succeeding one. Waste no time with outside men or topics, but adhere to your programme religiously. One or two good helpers from abroad are sufficient, and do not invite men out of compliment. Guard well all denominational interests and feelings. Draw together in harmony and conciliate. Never become opinionated or dogmatic, for the moment we cease to learn, our usefulness will decline. Give change, variety and life to all the exercises.

Finally, the spirituality of any Sunday-school gathering must be earnestly sustained, or all will be in vain. God alone can make a good superintendent, or a good Sabbath-school teacher. We are as nothing. The cause only is great. Therefore, with the Word of God in our hands, let *all things* be done in a sense of real heartfelt dependence upon God, and with earnest, believing supplication for the Divine direction and blessing.

Many of our Sabbath-school Conventions and Institutes are now very properly asssuming a mixed character, combining whatever is wanted of both, in every meeting. We need to arouse, instruct and train; and also to know the details of "how to do it." May the Master control all these gatherings to His glory and the good of man!

Rules.

1. Draw out the people to explain their wants, experience, and difficulties.

2. Then supply their wants.

3. Get one conductor, pay his expenses, and assign him to a good, quiet, comfortable place of entertainment near the church.

4. Commence promptly, and keep strictly to the programme and to time.

The following programme of an Institute we think most useful. It should be sent out two to four weeks in advance of the time of meeting:

PROGRAMME.

Tuesday Evening.

7 to 7.30, Religious conference and prayer for the Institute—two or three minute exercises.

7.30 to 7.40, Organization and miscellaneous business.

7.40 to 8, Sketch of progress and present position of the Sabbath-schools.

8 to 8.30, Brief reports from the counties or towns of their condition and destitution.

8.30 to 9, Instruction how to reach the neglected with schools, importance of illustrations, etc.

9 to 9.30, Review, with questions and answers.

Wednesday Morning.

9 to 9.20, Devotion—prayer for the schools.

9.20 to 9.50, Teachers' meetings by the Institute; how conducted, etc.

9.50 to 10.30, Review and instruction, by the conductor.

10.30 to 11, Black-board and its uses, by the Institute.

11 to 12, Review and instruction, by the conductor.

Wednesday Afternoon.

2 to 2.20, Devotional: prayer for the scholars.

2.20 to 2.40, Object-teaching, by the Institute.

2.40 to 3.20, Review and instruction, by the conductor.

3.20 to 3.40, Infant classes; how taught and difficulties.

3.40 to 4.30, Review and instruction; examples, etc., by the conductor.

4.30 to 5, Questions; box opened and answers given.

Wednesday Evening.

7 to 7.20, Conference and prayer for superintendents.

7.20 to 8, Superintending, opening exercises, and the library by the Institute—four speakers, ten minutes each.

8 to 9, Review and instruction, by the conductor.

9 to 9.30, Questions and answers.

Thursday Morning.

9 to 9.20, Conference and prayer for teachers.

9.20 to 10, How you teach; examples, modes, difficulties, etc., by the Institute.

10 to 11, Review and instruction; systems and modes of teaching.

11 to 12, Model-lessons, examples of teaching, etc.

Thursday Afternoon.

2 to 2.20, Conference and prayer for parents.

2.20 to 3.20, Divide the Institute into six classes, to be taught half an hour by six teachers; then have reports from these teachers, and criticism by the Institute.

3.20 to 3.35, Bible geography, maps, history, etc., by the Institute.

3.35 to 4, Examples, instructions, etc., by the conductor.

4 to 5, Questions and answers generally, on all subjects.

Thursday Evening.

7 to 7.30, Conference and prayer for conversions, the Church, etc.

7.30 to 8.10, Enlisting the church in Sabbath-school work; conversion and training of children, by the conductor; four speeches, ten minutes each, to the point, "how to do it."

8.10 to 9, Review of all by the conductor.

9 to 9.30, Closing addresses of five minutes each.

If no meeting is held on Tuesday evening, then drop out Thursday afternoon's exercises, and close up with the others. It is of the utmost importance that the pastors, superintendents, and teachers attend *all the exercises.* The Institute has an opportunity on every topic. Perhaps some pastor will favor with a model-lesson or drill-exercises on the subjects presented.

We need "line upon line" on some very important points, and, therefore, it is hoped that the *repetition* of some of these subjects in these articles will prove useful to many.

V.

THE SUPERINTENDENT.

HE whole character and influence of a Sabbath-school will depend largely upon the character and adaptedness of the superintendent. What the superintendent of a railroad, or the superintendent of a factory, or the commander of an army is, each in his place, so is the superintendent to his Sabbath-school. It is not every truly good and pious man, nor even every talented or eloquent man, who will make a good superintendent of a Sabbath-school. Sometimes the modest and retiring person, who shrinks from the acceptance of so holy an office, makes the best superintendent. Neither is it always the wisest or most influential man whom the office wants, but the one who can the most readily command the confidence and co-operation of the pastor, parents and church members, as well as the teachers and the children. Of course, the *best* man in the church, next to the pastor, should always be prayerfully called to the office, for it is difficult to

raise a Sabbath-school higher than its superintendent.

The superintendent should have good executive, business talents; energy; perseverance; self-control; tact to govern; a love for children; devotion to the cause; a warm, sympathetic heart; a life-like, serious, yet cheerful manner; and, superadded to humble, ardent piety, an ability to think, and to set others to thinking; and withal, he should be able to express himself clearly, briefly, and forcibly. He should never allow the least harsh or irritable expression to escape from him, and he should repress every symptom of lightness, stiffness, or discouragement, remembering that his look and manner will give tone to the whole school.

He should know personally, and by name, and as far as may be, the particular character of every teacher and pupil in the school; speak to them, and always treat them with confidence and respect—neither too coldly, nor too familiarly—and assure them each of his *personal* interest in them, and respect for them all.

He should be wise to discern, select, and adjust proper teachers to their places, classify and arrange the scholars, and in these things he should not be overborne in his judgment. He is usually chosen by the teachers annually, and will do well to take them for his counsellors, and often consult them, collectively and individually; for while he is the superintendent, the head of the school, and as such a cheerful obedience should be tendered to him by all, yet, he is *not the sovereign.* His authority is not magisterial nor parental, but he is a *constitutional* ruler, governed himself by the rules of the school; and he should so rule that no one should ever question his right to govern. He should never even speak of his "rights."

He should be *spiritually qualified* for his work, and should become a holier man of God from the hour in which he first receives the "call." He should be in daily communion with God about the work, talking freely with Him on all that concerns the school, about every teacher, and about every scholar, and humbly watching for answers to his prayers.

He should also engage in the work with a good measure of scriptural *enthusiasm.* We do well to be very earnest and full of life, to be glowing and animated in our looks, words, and actions, if we would effectually reach the children, who are so full of life. Perhaps the word unction would more worthily express the idea. The superintendent's interest should rise to this high point.

He should maintain good *discipline and order*, both for himself and his school. Sometimes the most disorderly man in the whole school is the superintendent. The two elements of good order are self-control and good temper. Let no man think he can control others unless he can control himself. It will be in vain for him to insist on order, punctuality, and regard to all the rules of the school, unless he himself is a living example of strict conformity to them all. When he calls the school to order, let him always wait patiently, in silence, until every teacher, every scholar, officer and visitor, is in *perfect* order, before he names a hymn or proceeds to do the least thing.

He should also be *disinterested*, and never overshadow his teachers. They are the great workers, and his great work is to help the teachers in the teaching. He should not *forestall* or *overshadow* the teacher's work by an exposition of the lesson at the opening of the school, so as to leave the teachers nothing to do but to glean after the superintendent. His remarks and reviews of the lesson should usually come *after* the teachers have taught the lesson.

He should likewise *sincerely respect* all his teachers, and treat them accordingly. Especially should he respect the weakest and most inefficient of his teachers. He will have the more to do to aid them, and he must needs visit, counsel, suggest and instruct them often. I have always found it better to elevate and improve inefficient teachers than to dismiss them.

The superintendent should also be a man of good *executive ability;* and this is a very rare possession. He needs much discerning power, as well as organizing and combining talent, so as to keep pastor and people, parents, teachers, and scholars, all harmoniously at work. As Dr. James W. Alexander used to say: "That man who can well superintend a Sabbath-school can command an army;" and a well-known bishop has said, that "the man who can organize a good mission-school can organize a diocese."

Again: The Sunday-school superintendent should always have a *spirit and temper* such as will be safe to diffuse throughout the school. Says the Rev. S. Martin: "If he stands at the desk like a cold, snow-capped mountain, or floats about the school like a majestic iceberg, the whole atmosphere of the school will be cold." If he is warm and genial, such will be the school. A cheerful superintendent spreads cheerfulness throughout the school. A light and trifling, or a gloomy and morose, superintendent infects teachers and scholars alike with the same spirit. Never should the superintendent allow the least impatience or harshness to manifest itself in his look, tone of voice, or manner in the school; for its effects will prove most disastrous. Ill-temper is a perfect barrier to religious improvement and usefulness.

He should also be a decided, *positive* character; not fitful, obstinate, heady, but strong in purpose, strong in resolution, strong in the Lord. The boys in the streets never choose any but positive characters for leaders. A merely nominal superintendent is a curse to a school, as is a weak, foolish mother, or father, in the family.

Further, he should study to gather hints and suggestions to help the teachers not only in the school, but also in the teachers' meetings and everywhere.

Particularly should he observe the teachers during the teaching hour, and never interrupt them, but be ready at any moment to come to their assistance. He should always *protect* the teachers while teaching, and not allow the librarian, or secretary, or missionary collector, to appear on the floor at that time.

It will be seen from these points that the superintendent needs great *general strength of character.* Willow will do for a basket, but it requires oak and iron for a man-of-war. Never are the teachers called to a more important duty than when they prayerfully cast their votes for the election of superintendent. No personal favoritism or interest or prejudice should be allowed for a single moment to prevail.

If I am here asked, "Do you know of any such superintendents as are here described?" I must reply in the negative. I have endeavored to embody in the above list of qualifications all the best things of the best superintendents whom I have seen during the last forty-five years. Nevertheless, the things which are here detailed have their counterparts in some of them. The standard is raised high, so that the true artist can copy after the great masters. Let none be discouraged. The best superintendents now living were very distrustful of their qualifications, and shrank from the responsibility at the first call. If God calls a man to a field of labor, he is abundantly competent to fit him for working in it. Then "not unto us, O Lord, not unto us, but unto thy name give glory."

Duties of the Superintendent.

Let us look now at some of the *duties* of the good Sabbath-school superintendent.

Before school he will, of course, prepare his mind, by meditation and prayer, for his duties; he will faithfully study the lesson, select the hymns and Scripture lesson for the day, and carefully read them and study them, until he has imbibed so much of their spirit as to be able to *feel* them, and to express that feeling while reading them before the school. He will, also, prepare his notices, and arrange for all special duties. All the teachers, with the superintendent, ought to enjoy a twenty-minute prayer-meeting before the hour to open the school, with two-minute direct prayers, one or two verses of singing at a time, and then only one or two selections of warm, appropriate verses of Scripture truth. We would characterize the requirements of such a meeting by these words—*Impressive*, *Interesting*, *Devout.*

The Opening Exercises.—The good superintendent will always be punctual in opening, and at the precise minute calmly, but clearly and naturally, call the school to order. Having done this, he will never proceed farther until every teacher, scholar, secretary, librarian, or visitor *is in order.* He will remember that every eye is on *him* for an example, and he will take no liberty himself with the rules of the school. When perfect silence and complete attention are gained, he will deliberately read the hymn and see tha all sing, about two or three verses; then read impres sively the lesson for the day, if not more than from te to fifteen verses, or alternate with the school in read ing if preferable. Be careful to mind all the stops and read in clear, impressive tones, so that the read ing of the Scriptures by the school will be almost a musical as singing. All will then unite in praye with the superintendent, one of the teachers, the pas tor, or a visitor present, who may be called upon this prayer should be short and to the point, and in short sentences and in children's language. Have the children join in and repeat the prayer, broken up into sentences of four or five words each. Thus teach the children how to pray. The whole of the opening exercises should not usually exceed fifteen minutes. The school will then be given into the hands of the teachers, to proceed with the lesson.

During Teaching.—The superintendent will then quietly supply every vacant class with a teacher, or unite it with another class which has a teacher, so that every scholar may be placed at once, temporarily, at least, in charge of some one, and that no one may be suffered to be idle. Next, he will check off the names of teachers present on his roll-book; and then proceed to receive the new scholars, learn their names, residence, parents; gain their confidence; ascertain whether they do not now belong to some other good school; inform them of the character and order of the Sunday-school, and assign them a place, temporary or permanent, in a class. He will then pass quietly and discreetly around the room, recognizing the teachers and scholars as far as may be, without interrupting or embarrassing them, assisting any teacher who may need it to restore order and harmony, or to gain the attention of any volatile youth in the class. With the approval of the teacher, he will occasionally examine the class, notice all disturbing elements in the school, the adaptedness, or otherwise, of the teachers for the particular classes in their charge; occasionally recommending and handing an appropriate book from the library to a teacher or scholar, and calling especial attention to it for their profit. The Bible classes and infant classes will be timely noticed, and all strangers and visitors greeted with a courteous, Christian welcome. Suitable suggestions will be made to the secretary and librarian; any call for assistance or explanation will be given to any teacher; and thus, in every appropriate, unobtrusive way, he will do whatever he can to facilitate the work of all, while hindering none.

Superintendents should be very cautious whom they invite to address the school, and particularly strangers of whom they know but little, only that they are called very good men. Few persons can address a Sunday-school with profit; and certainly, without important reasons, the teachers should not be interrupted in their regular duties; for the time allotted to them is *theirs*, and even the superintendent has *no right* to take it to oblige a friend.

Closing the School.—At the appointed moment the superintendent will call the school again to order, to sing over a verse of a hymn in harmony with the lesson; and then the superintendent may occupy not to exceed five or ten minutes in a clear, well-digested exposition of, or some pertinent remarks or questions upon, the prominent points or teachings of the lesson. Unless he can succeed in interesting and fixing the attention of both teachers and scholars with thoughts not ordinarily dwelt upon by the teachers, he had better not attempt this exercise; for few evils are greater in a school than a superintendent who talks too much. Many of our best and most successful and acceptable superintendents never attempt to address their schools, except to give their notices and necessary directions in a clear, orderly, business-like way, and then stop at once. An opportunity is then given to distribute the library books and papers, give out the next week's lesson, sing a verse or two of the selected hymn, or with a prayer dismiss the school in regular order.

After the school the superintendent will receive any suggestions or requests from teachers or scholars; see that everything is left in its place; review the events of the school, and note down all his plans for improvement, and begin to study his next lesson.

During the week he will remember that his duties as superintendent do not close with the Sabbath, or monthly concert, or teachers' meeting. Every day he regards the Sabbath-school as his great field of labor in the moral vineyard. Let us follow him, and we shall see him on *Monday morning* on his way to his regular business, when as he meets little Johnny Smith, who, he remembers, was not in his place in school yesterday, he very pleasantly inquires the reason. On the corner of the next street he comes across an absent teacher, and similar inquiries ensue. On his return home at evening he sees in the distance, in company with a lot of street-girls, Mary Jones, and he hastens to her, takes her aside with him, and learns the reason of her leaving school some weeks before, together with other facts in her history, which call out kind words of caution for the wayward child, and he leaves her with the warm assurance of her return. In the evening he is at the monthly concert of prayer for Sabbath-schools, and drops a few earnest remarks about the children, which have such an effect upon two mothers present that they go home and become more faithful thenceforth in their Christian duty to their beloved little ones.

On the way, *Tuesday*, he stops in a few moments to see a teacher who appeared quite perplexed and disheartened on the Sabbath by the restlessness, inattention, or indifference of her class. He noticed last Sabbath that that teacher could only interest the class for a few minutes. On looking over the next week's lesson he is reminded of that teacher and one of her scholars. The next morning he calls for a moment upon her on his way to business, and says: "Miss S——, there is one verse of the lesson that I think can be used with advantage with one of your scholars—Frank Jones." He explains it to the teacher, and gives her an illustration or two. What has he done? He has given that teacher the first real idea she ever had of teaching Bible truth aright, and she goes to her class the next Sabbath a new teacher, and never loses the influence in future life. He soon succeeds in dispelling the cloud, and causing a cheerful light to shine on her path of duty.

On *Wednesday evening* he steps over to consult the pastor about the best way of turning the hearts of parents to their children, and to arouse the church in *sympathetic* efforts on behalf of the lambs of the flock.

On *Thursday morning* he takes an hour before, or an interval of business, to explore a desperate neighborhood, and succeeds beyond his expectations in exciting interest and enlisting recruits for the Sunday-school from among the juvenile portion of the disorderly gang. He also takes occasion to call on little Pat Lawless's mother, and is successful in getting her pledge to co-operate with him in the attempt to rescue her boy from untold depravity and almost certain ruin. Pat is notoriously the ringleader in the worst gang of boys in the neighborhood, and every body was surprised to see little Harry Page leading him into the Sunday-school for the first time on the last Sabbath morning.

On his way back from business, *Friday* evening, he calls for a few minutes on an intelligent young Christian who recently came into the place, in order to seek his Christian acquaintance, and invite him to look up for himself a class of scholars from the neglected neighborhood he visited the day before, and he succeeds in inducing him to bring into the school and teach a fine class of street-boys the way of life; he takes a hint from the conversation with his young friend, and concludes to get up a neat printed certificate of reward to the pupils for bringing in new scholars. In the weekly prayer-meeting he has a word about the school, just enough to enlist their sympathies and their prayers.

Saturday morning, on opening the daily paper or a book, he sees a striking providence, an interesting fact or incident of life, which, he remembers at once, will aptly illustrate or enforce an important truth in the lesson for the next Sabbath, and carefully notes it down and *thinks* it over, and in the evening we find him full of hope and interest at the teachers' meeting. Thus closes his labors for the week. It is *only* a week! but how valuable is that life of which this is but a week!

Now, all this is no mere fancy sketch. We have had living superintendents—not *one* but all together—sitting for the portrait here drawn, and whose lives have supplied all the illustrations, and who pursue a somewhat similar course every week, and on every returning Sabbath-day. Thus, without scarcely an hour's interference with his duties to his family, his business, or the public, the good superintendent has found time, and has been enabled every day during the week, to do something for the Sunday-school, simply because he loves it; his heart is on it, and he loves constantly to devise ways of doing good by it. He never expects to be, and he never will be, satisfied with the school as it is; but, however great the progress, he will keep his mind actively at work to plan improvements in the arrangement, the order, the discipline, the enterprise, or the teaching, and thus, *Upward and Onward*, will be his perpetual motto.

A stagnant business, he knows, will soon droop and die.

VI.

THE LIBRARY AND LIBRARIAN.

E have a very high appreciation of the value of a good Sabbath-school library. It seems to me that no form of circulating sound religious reading is superior. The books, however, require to be selected and adapted with the greatest care. This is certainly a difficult matter, but the object to be attained is so great as to reward the effort. Many schools are now flooded with the most vicious, improper books. There is no justifiable excuse for this. Never were there so many good books for children and youth as now. Several hundreds that teach the soundest Christian morals and are true to life, and filled with the soundest evangelical Bible instruction, can now be selected. There is scarcely a shadow of excuse at the present time for admitting even a doubtful book into our Sabbath-school libraries—unless some will accept the plea of ignorance and laziness. Our children's minds should be as sacredly guarded from poisonous books as their bodies from poisonous drugs. There should be a judicous standing committee in every school to select library books,

while the pastor should always carefully revise their selection.

The books of the Sabbath-school library must be attractive and interesting, or they will not be read by the young. They must be true to life and fact, or they will prove pernicious. They must be instructive, or they should find no place in the library. They should be adapted to awaken, convict and convert, to nourish in the religious life and morals, and throw light upon all the pathway of everyday practical life, or they will fall short of meeting the great want. They must strictly conform in all things to the Bible standard, or they should never be found in any of our Sabbath-school libraries.

Better have no books than to have unsound ones. Spare no pains to procure an abundance of good, sound, attractive, and useful reading, and we will soon drive away the flood of bad books which is now threatening to destroy our youth. *Several copies* of superior books should be placed in the library at the same time. Select such as are adapted to all ages and conditions, from the children in the infant-school up to the wide-awake young men and women in our highest adult Bible classes, and to teachers. Let them also cover all stages of religious feeling and want. Books of narrative, history, biography, youthful Christian experience and training, on temperance, good morals, good habits and manners, should all be provided for the thorough religious instruction of our children and youth. The library should also comprise a good teacher's library with good reference Bibles, a Concordance and Dictionary. Then give the books the largest, freest and most active circulation.

Managing the Library.—In a great many Sabbath-schools the manner of distributing the books is a very bad one, and in consequence of this some schools have improperly discarded the library altogether. The great difficulty has arisen from the fact that the librarian has been allowed to be on the floor and have access to and interrupt the teachers during the teaching hour. This should never be allowed. An interruption to the teacher while applying divine truth may peril souls for ever, and therefore should be carefully guarded. The only access to the teachers which the librarian ought to be allowed during school hours is to simply hand them the books, just at the close of school. There are several good systems for distributing the books that conform to this idea and protect the teachers. I would never ask the teachers to write the scholars' names or numbers for books, or do the work of selection, during the school hours.

In the management of the library, what is called "The Check System" is considered one of the best. We cannot describe the various good plans, but I will detail one which seems to me to be more simple and to obviate more difficulties than any other that I am acquainted with. It first provides a carefully-printed numerical catalogue of all the books, with the number of pages. Give to each scholar one of these catalogues, and replace it when lost. If the school is a small district-school, a written catalogue will answer the purpose equally well. Then a "Library Card," four inches by two-and-a-half inches, is provided for each scholar on the first of each month. On this is written or printed—"Library Card," "Class No. 6," "John Smith." Each scholar takes his "Library Card" and catalogue home, and there, with aid from his parents or a friend, he selects from ten to fifteen books, either of which he will be satisfied with during the next four weeks. The "Library Card" is then placed in his book, and kept there as a marker, and is returned to the librarian on the next Sabbath with the book. Each scholar hands his book, with the card in it, as he enters the room, to the librarian, who is always to be found at the opening of the school at the outer door of the school-room, with a large basket ready to receive all the books from the pupils. When the school is opened the librarian carries these books to the library and assorts them, as he ascertains from each book-mark to whom and what class and name the book belongs. The book is then credited as returned, and the new one charged. If any scholar wants one book particularly that is on his list, he *underscores* it, and if it is in the library, it is given to him and charged. If any scholar is late, and the librarian has gone to the library, he loses his exchange of books on that Sabbath. The librarian keeps the account of all library-books, and charges them all to each name and class according to the book-mark, and credits them when returned, and the teacher has no care of it. After the teaching is closed, the lesson reviewed by the superintendent, remarks made, prayer, singing, etc., then the librarian, by a notice from the superintendent, passes down the aisle and hands each teacher his lot of books, and the teacher passes them to each pupil according to the library card, and then the school is dismissed. No scholar opens his library-book or paper in the school. The teachers have no care of the books or their numbers, unless the scholar loses his library-card; in which case his teacher, at the close of the school, accompanies him to the library and obtains for him a new library-card and book. The librarian and his assistant charge and credit all the books while the teachers are teaching. Each class has a column or place in the register. This plan satisfies the scholar, he has his own choice, and never interrupts the teachers or the school for a moment, or diverts the attention of the school, and no time is lost. It works admirably.

The Librarian.—The librarian's office is an important one. He should be one of the most considerate, watchful, careful young men in all the community, for his office gives him much prominence. He should open the library, arrange it in order, distribute hymn and class-books before the school opens, and allow no unauthorized person access to the library. He will become acquainted with the general character of the books, as well as know the scholars, that he may intelligently aid them in their selections. He will, also, ascertain what class of books is most in demand.

VII.

THE SECRETARY.

HIS indispensable officer of the school is a sort of clerk or helper to the superintendent.

1. He should be a good accountant, prompt, watchful and attentive. He should keep a record of the attendance.

2. He should make a note of the opening exercises, with the names of those who participate, and any interesting circumstances connected with them.

3. He should record the names of all the scholars and teachers who have been or are now connected with the school, and note everything of their changes in life and history; especially their profession of religion, marriage, etc.—keeping up a correspondence with them. This record-book will become very valuable as the years roll on, since it includes parents' names, every removal and death, etc., etc.

4. He will also count the number of scholars and teachers present, enter it in the minute-book, and note the absentees.

5. He should write up the class-books, and deliver them to the teachers.

6. He should enter in the minute-book the names of visitors, especially if the pastor be one of them; note the addresses, what kind of weather, and all items affecting the school.

7. He should give certificates of dismissal to every teacher or scholar about removing to another place, recommending them to the Christian fellowship of those who love Christ's lambs.

8. He should know every scholar, so that he can check them off without asking the teacher the name, and should have a quick, vigilant eye, not only for his own duties, but, also, in order to communicate valuable suggestions respecting the school to the superintendent.

9. In the absence of the superintendent, he may sometimes take his place in the charge of the school, except in the case of very large schools, which may require an assistant to the superintendent.

VIII.

THE TEACHER.

THE true Sabbath-school teacher is one called and "sent of God;" for we read (1 Cor. xii. 28), "And God hath set some in the church, first apostles, secondarily prophets, thirdly *teachers;*" and the same divine lips which said "Go preach," said also "Go teach." Whosoever receives this sacred call should devote himself to it by a holy consecration, remembering that he is truly an ambassador from the King of kings to a small circle of his rebellious subjects,—a ransomed sinner offering pardon to precious youth condemned to die. His great business is the preparation of young immortals for the kingdom of heaven through the application of heaven-revealed truth by a simple appeal to their intelligence and feelings through the power of the Holy Spirit. This is truly an angel's errand entrusted to redeemed sinners. Mr. Groser justly says: "The office of a Christian teacher transcends all others in interest and importance. No matter what his precise sphere of labor may be, whether that of a professor like Chalmers, a pastor like Oberlin, a schoolmaster like

Arnold, or a Sunday-school teacher like the 300,000 men and women who on each returning Sabbath seek to instruct our youth in those truths which are able to make them wise unto salvation." He should, therefore, accept his mission thankfully, and enter upon it heartily, and attend to his duties punctually, faithfully, and earnestly.

He is to teach Bible truth. That is the divinely provided aliment for the human mind, and if rightly taught and received it will be attractive and satisfying to the soul, and all besides will be only supplementary. To be able to teach Bible truth thus faithfully and truly, calls for *hard*, *earnest* work, for, says one of the English bishops, "It takes all we know to make things plain." The teacher, therefore, must needs be well furnished and thoroughly fitted for his high calling.

This brings us to the next article, on the teacher's preparation.

IX.

PREPARATION.

HE work of teaching divine truth is so difficult and important that every teacher should do himself the justice to make the most clear and careful preparation. No teacher can impart more than he has prepared to teach, and he should therefore bring to his class only beaten oil, well-digested and well-adapted thoughts, something worthy of being taught, and that will command attention for their own sake. It is well for the teacher to have method and system, as well as a set time and place to begin that preparation. The time to commence, we think, should be on the afternoon or evening of the previous Sabbath, and the place in the quiet of the home circle or the study.

1. Pray and read, and read and *think* and PRAY over the lesson; the words and the spirit of it. Here look for the best thoughts to use.

2. Search the Scriptures with the aid of a Concordance, or good reference Bible, for the most pointed and practical parallel passages and references; they will wonderfully illuminate the lesson.

3. By aid of the Bible references, and a good dictionary, be careful to get the clear, exact meaning of the important words of the lesson, in words adapted to your class.

4. Next use your Teachers' Helps, Commentaries, Bible Geographies, Bible Dictionaries, Maps, Antiquities, etc.

5. Go out into the world and gather excellent things for illustration of the Bible truth from what you see, hear, read or do.

6. Visit your scholars' homes in the preparation of your lessons, and learn their peculiar trials and temptations. Study well your children, child-nature and child-language, "Peep of Day" and "Line upon Line" are pure specimens of child-language.

7. Get something for *each* pupil, for Johnny is not at all like Willy, and Willy is not like Charlie, etc. Break up Bible truths into small pieces for the children and youth. Do not wander afar for simile, but remember "knowledge is *before* him that understandeth, but the eyes of a fool are in the ends of the earth."

8. Make full notes, write out your facts and references, etc.: (*a*) Of your best thoughts. (*b*) Of your best plan of teaching. (*c*) The aim and object of the lesson illustrations. (*d*) Of the commencement and closing of the teaching lesson.

9. Think it all over so carefully and repeatedly that you will need scarcely to look at the notes to the end. Select just what to teach, and do not stuff the

children. Memorize the lesson and you will have special unction in teaching.

10. Prepare more, far more, than you will want to use, that you may have ample material for selections; for no teacher can impart all that he is prepared to teach, and the teacher should be careful NEVER TO EXHAUST HIMSELF.

Finally. Do not be tied down to any one plan or method of preparing a Sabbath lesson, but invent new and fresh modes. Never suffer any part of your preparation or teaching to relapse into a dull routine. Be fresh, warm, and earnest in manner and matter, and raise yourself above leaning upon any question-books or notes of lessons; use them if you please, but do not lean upon them. The weekly teachers'-meeting is an indispensable assistant to every faithful teacher. Never forget that the only sort of knowledge which can answer a Sabbath-school teacher's purpose "must be at once thorough, detailed, abundant, and exact."

It is of the first importance that the teacher of children should study well child-nature, child-language, and all the child's characteristics—such as activity, curiosity, inquisitiveness, etc.; what are its wants and cares; its dangers and its duties; its hopes and fears; its sympathies and feelings, likes and dislikes. All these must be candidly considered if we would prepare for the position of Christian counsellor and guide to the child. We must gain its confidence, draw out its sympathies, and win its heart, and all this will require the most diligent, earnest, prayerful study. In this process the teacher must needs often recall his own childhood, and live that over again—become as a little child again—if he would become a child's teacher. Do not ever fall into the error of supposing that your children are ever too young or too ignorant to appreciate a well-prepared lesson.

After these very full directions for the *teacher*, I am here permitted by Mr. Ralph Wells to give the notes of his actual *superintendent's* preparation in the regular service of Grace Mission-school, only one week before the previous part of this article was written. The following are his exact notes:

"THE SUPERINTENDENT'S PREPARATION."

Subject—*Hypocrisy.*

Time, 8 hours' *intense* study.

Commenced Sabbath evening previous.

1. Prayer for light. Do YOU?

2. Go to the Bible to see what it says.

3. Texts found. *Write all out.* Job xx. 5; xxvii. 8–10; xxxvi. 13, 14. Prov. xxx. 12. Psalms lxv. 2–5. Ezek. xxxiii. 31, 32. Matt. vi. 2; xxiv. 51. Luke xii. 1. Mark xii. 15.

4. *Definition of Hypocrisy.*

To seek to appear what I am not.

5. Bible Examples.

	Causes.	End.
Saul, 1 Sam. xv. 14.	Love of gain.	—
Gehazi, 2 Kings, v. 26.	"	—
Judas, Matt. xxvi. 50.	"	—
Ananias, Acts v. 1–26.	Gain and applause.	—
Simon Magus, Acts viii. 26.	Gain.	—
Absalom, 2 Sam. xv. 1–12.	Power.	—

6. Look into the lesson and examples until I *feel* it myself.

7. Emblems.

Bible.	Common.
Leaven.	The mask.
Whited sepulchres.	Counterfeit money.
Hidden graves.	Paste jewels.
Spider's web.	

8. Common ways for all ages.

The store, the bank, and the office.
Profession of religion for credit.
Political, on 'change, fashionable, flattering.

9. Children's Dangers.

Don't tell mother.
Boy getting my white-alley.
Desire to please teachers or gain praise.
The hypocrite lies with his hands, face, clothes, gifts.

10. *Illustrations.*

Photograph—Absalom's monument.
Friar—Nelly and love of Jesus.
Picture of a hypocritical saint—London beggar.

11. *Absalom's double face to his father and to God.*

Picture the scene. 2 Sam. xv. 1–13.

12. *Hypocrisy.*

Its meaning.	Its causes.
Its folly.	Its end.

The simple notes certainly give but a faint idea of how thoroughly hypocrisy is unmasked in this lesson. The teacher or scholar will never forget it. "*Intense* study" should be contrasted with the *easy*-chair, lounging, intermitting study of many.

"The store, the bank," etc., refer to rum shops; so named that husbands and young men who return at late hours may say, I have just left "*the bank*," etc.

The "photograph of Absalom's monument" reminds us that, to this day, every Jew casts a stone at it, and curses the hypocrite's memory; and so on with the other illstrations.

The following brief notes were taken at one of our New York Association's meetings: Subject—How to prepare a Sabbath-school lesson. "Piety *alone* is not what we want in Sabbath-school teaching any more than preaching." Take the lesson—Luke xviii. 35—"A certain blind man," etc. Take a good Reference Bible and a Bible Dictionary.

I ask myself, What is in this passage? A miracle. Say something about miracles, but never lead a child into deep water. I can never make a thing plain to another that I cannot make plain to myself. You cannot teach more than you can put into words, etc.

Tell them about a particular part of the country Jericho (Josh. ii., and 2 Kings xvi. 34), sixteen miles from Jerusalem, and about six from the river Jordan. I find here a beggar—*two*, but one is silent. "Jesus, thou Son of David"—the sublime epithet applied to the Messiah. His suit is for mercy. "Cried the *more*"—evidence of faith—plea for mercy—earnestness. Jesus is arrested in his progress by the prayer of the needy man. Prayer arrests all laws. Jesus stood and commanded. You have got to come to Jesus. Submission to Jesus absolutely essential. What wilt thou? We are to tell Christ just what we want. Prayer is absolutely necessary. Jesus made the blind man tell Him. Revive thy faith. Must believe. How apply. What last impressions to leave. Jesus was going up to Jerusalem for the last time. Only opportunity, or last opportunity. All go. This opportunity, dear boys, may be the last.

The superintendent, as well as the teachers, needs the most ample and careful preparation of the lesson, in order to suggest and aid and sympathize with the teachers and school, and to conduct the teachers' meeting.

X.

THE TEACHER TEACHING.

HE teacher is the master and superior, and his character, attitude, bearing and words should be well calculated to govern and to guide. Teaching is not simply educating—namely, drawing out, nor simply instructing the pupil, but *training* him. It is taking my thought and converting it to *his use.*

With this view great care should be taken to begin a lesson aright. The teacher should come from communion with God, and his spirit and manner should be at once thoughtful, earnest and cheerful, never cold, cheerless, indifferent, or severe. Let him give to each scholar a warm, quiet, but hearty salutation; be early, be calm, be gentle, be firm and seriously in earnest; never allow any scholar to take any undue liberties; and see that each one and everything is in its place.

With interest and reverence the teacher and his class will then enter upon the devotional opening exercises, joining in them. After which he will gather his class around him, and first place himself on terms of good-will with all, and find some *common ground* for their minds to begin acting upon. A well-timed, easy, and awakening question about the former or present lesson will arrest attention, but it must be well adapted, and readily answered. The first questions must never perplex or embarrass the pupil, for they are very important. From thence proceed and rapidly draw their minds up towards the great central thought of the lesson; awakening thought, arousing curiosity, and deepening impressions.

The teacher should question the lesson *out* of the pupils, and then question it *into* them. He will first get the *words* of the lesson clearly into the minds of the scholars—mostly by catechising—and then the *meaning* and illustration of the principal words. Next the *lessons* of instruction must be carefully drawn, and lastly, *applied* to the heart and life of all.

A severe test comes upon the teacher in the recitation and catechising upon the lesson. He is to remember: 1. To draw all the information that he can from the class; 2. To induce the class to find out all they can for themselves; 3. To give such information as is best for the class, but before giving any information, be sure that no member of the class *can* give it.

The true teacher starts from the *known*, and proceeds over short and easy stepping-stones to the faintly known, thence to the contrast, and then to the unknown. Some very learned men utterly fail as teachers.

They take such tremendous strides that no pupil can follow them. It is like the father rushing up three steps at a time to the top of the staircase. If he would lead his child, he must be careful to take but one step at a time. Let the child's present knowledge be the starting-point for all future acquisitions. Reading, or even reciting, a lesson, may possibly teach nothing. "'Tis in vain that you make them read the life and doctrines of the Saviour, if you do not explain to them that he lived for their example, that he died to redeem them, and that those doctrines are to govern them in thought, word and deed." Care should be taken to select the best plan of arranging the lesson. "The *beginning* should arrest attention, the *middle* inform the mind, and the *end* affect the heart." Let there be a natural order and method in all your teaching;—one thought gliding into and connecting with the next, and so on. In no department of life is system and method of more value, and a child is as much aided by it as a man. Robertson justly says: "Memory without method is useless. Detached facts are practically valueless." Method is the laying out of the lesson and proceeding in its natural order in conformity with the uniform laws of the human mind. It tells what shall come first and second, and puts everything in its right place, so that the mind can take a clearer grasp, and memory a more easy and a more retentive hold, of the truths presented.

We should not, however, bind ourselves to any *one* method of teaching, for there is no standard mode alike adapted to different persons and lessons. The most of our good teachers have wrought out some way of teaching in a measure peculiar to themselves and adapted to them. Those who can do so, however, will be able to borrow much of value from "Gall's Lesson System," with its thorough analysis, numerous exercises, exhaustive doctrines and lessons of instruction, or from "Stow's Training System," with its sympathy of numbers, its picturing out into life and training which will aid others, and "Mimpriss's Gospel Harmony" will help many. Let us ride no hobbies, but gather the best suggestions from all for our Sabbath-school work.

What we want in our Sabbath-schools is to add a sufficiency of teaching-power—to give efficacy to our teaching without stiffening it with rules and forms.

A few years ago hymn-learning, catechism, and task-lessons formed the staple of even our Scripture-classes. Now there is a demand for good Bible-teaching, that will equal the teaching of our best academies and colleges. The Bible is so adapted and wonderful as to place us on great vantage ground. We want to know, How to use it? Mr. J. G. Fitch, of the Normal College, London, has given us an admirable synopsis of the few simple principles which underlie the great art, and which, as he justly observes, "require to be pondered and thoroughly grasped by every teacher:"

1. "Never to teach what you do not quite un-

derstand." Clear knowledge makes clear, pleasant teaching.

2. "Never to tell a child what you could make that child tell you." He will thus remember it ten times as long.

3. "Never to give a piece of information without asking for it again." The mind cannot retain what it does not expect to be called on for again, or to have a future use for.

4. "Never to use a hard word if an easy one will convey your meaning; and never to use any word at all unless you are quite sure that it has a meaning to convey." Mark—not "long" word, but "hard" word.

5. "Never to begin an address, or a lesson, without a clear view of its end." Then aim high and at the mark.

6. "Never to give an unnecessary command, nor one which you do not mean to see obeyed." Therefore, few commands; for in case you fail to secure obedience the child rules you, and not you the child.

7. "Never to permit a child to remain in the class for a minute without something to do, and a motive for doing it." A child wants something to do, and cannot bear to be idle. Keep him busy.

Teaching is an art, and like any other art, it has to be learned—learned, too, by study, observation, and practice. It has its rules and principles. He who knows and practises them is a good workman; while he who neglects them is necessarily inefficient.

First, we must get the ideas and *principles*. Secondly, we must *imitate* or copy the good examples or models; and thirdly, we are to practise teaching; for the best way to learn how to teach is to *teach*. Said Ralph Wells, when asked how he learned to teach, "By my mistakes and failures." In teaching others successfully we teach ourselves effectively.

In seeking after our models or examples to copy, we need not, like the artist, go to Italy in order to copy the great masters; for the great Master of teaching—Christ, our Model Teacher and the teacher's model—is always before us, and His example is perfect. He is "the Teacher come from God." "He spake as never man spake." Let us notice some characteristics of His teaching:

1. He was *very instructive*. He knew what was in man, and just how to meet his wants. If our words do not instruct, they "are simply impertinent." Do our "lips teach knowledge?"

2. He was *beautifully simple*,—child-like, but never childish; so clear that all could understand. So our words should be few, well-chosen, simple, and adapted, softly and deliberately expressed.

3. His teaching was *highly illustrative*. So should ours be. He gathered from all the common surroundings of life. The tiny sparrow was made to illustrate His care; He pointed the magi to the stars; the fishermen were to be fishers of men; He taught a lesson to the merchant-man from the goodly pearl; the water-bearer was offered the water of life;

while the wheat, the grain, the tares, the chaff, the vine, the tree, the field, and almost every object taught the husbandman amid his daily toil. Heaven itself is represented by earthly things and objects the most valued—by "songs," "arches," "harps of gold," "rivers clear as crystal," "rivers of pleasure," "pearly gates," "precious rubies and stones," etc. His illustrations always threw *light* upon truth—never *displaced* it, as ours sometimes do. They were drawn from everyday life, and so well adapted that they were joyfully received by the candid inquirer. Let all Sabbath-school teachers herein copy the Master. Apt illustrations render truth more permanent; for it is well said, that the "simile, the anecdote, the fable, is sure to be remembered, and the sentiment to which it was linked is sure to go with it."

4. His teaching was, also, *sublimely courageous.* "He spake as one having authority." His confidence in God and in His truth raised Him above fear and doubt.

5. His teaching was *singularly adapted.* It always reached the heart and life.

6. His teaching was *mingled with prayer.* He went out to teach; He retired to pray. Let all teachers imitate His example.

7. His teaching was *closely applied.* Let our teaching, also, be carried home to the everyday life of the children, and applied closely, particularly, personally, and privately to specific errors and sins;

for we never should allow ourselves for a moment to doubt that there is no infirmity in manner or purpose, in habit, temper, or character, amongst our children, which the Sunday-school, with its divine text-book, is not abundantly competent to reach and remove.

Sabbath-school teaching should combine at least—1. The art of asking questions. 2. Keeping order. 3. The art of securing attention and interesting the pupils. 4. The drawing of practical lessons and applying them to the daily, common life. We should never undertake to teach a truth of which we cannot see and make plain its uses; certainly never convey to our children the idea that there is any unimportant portion of revealed truth. One or two Bible-truths and principles are generally better than many.

The art of drawing lessons is much more simple and easy even for children than most persons think. The only prerequisites for drawing practical lessons are—1. A knowledge of the facts. 2. An accurate perception whether they be good or evil. If the action or precept be good, the practical lesson is but an echo of the fact; if evil, avoid. Imitate the good and shun the evil. For instance: Cain and Abel were industrious; from which we learn the duty to be industrious. Cain and Abel went up to worship God; from which learn to copy their good example in going to worship God. But Cain became angry and slew his brother; from which we draw the lesson of warning and danger.

Another important part of a teacher's work may be found in Mr. Fitch's third rule, *i. e.*, Every teacher before he leaves the lesson, should carefully call back in a child's own language all that he has taught him Without this careful, thorough review and *recapitu lation* he cannot be sure that his instructions and the practical lessons taught are really received. A child is, as it were, compelled to remember what he is sure to be called upon for again; so that we can hardly overestimate the value of review and recapitu lation. One superintendent in New York recently reviewed, by aid of a black-board, the whole of John's Gospel with his scholars on two consecutive Sabbaths. The teacher should keep his eyes upon all the class, and address the class generally more than the individual members of the class; but be ready to sympathize with each and all.

Never be in a hurry with the lesson; calmly, pa tiently, candidly proceed. It is far better to get the pupils to *understand* the first verse or a single thought of the lesson, and proceed no farther, than to hasten over a dozen verses.

Paul says: "I had rather speak five words with my understanding, that by *my voice* I might *teach* others also, than ten thousand words in an unknown tongue." (1 Cor. xiv. 19.) Be strictly impartial; have no favorites in the school; be tenderly respectful to the weaker ones. Particular care should be taken to preserve order fully until the *close* of the school, fo then it becomes most difficult; and after the schoo he will retire to his closet and commend his feeble, imperfect labors in prayer to God. He will ask himself the following questions: "Does any child leave me to-day with a clear, simple view of *one truth* of the gospel of Jesus Christ?" and, "Is it a matter perfectly understood between me and my pupils to-day that I am seeking their conversion to God at *this time*, and under my instructions?" He will then think over the events of the hour, and commence his preparation for his next lesson. During the week the Sabbath-school teacher will find something to do every day. On one evening he will visit an absentee, or look up a new scholar; on another, visit some of the parents; then attend a social meeting, or the teachers' meeting, and on another call to interest one to become a new teacher. He gets one boy a place to work, and another he introduces into the public school; gives his scholars his name and residence on a card, and endeavors in all ways to prove himself to be a warm-hearted, sympathizing Christian friend.

The teacher's life is the life of his teaching. His character, manners, habits, dress, and associations, all exert an influence of great power upon his pupils and upon his fellow-teachers; and he will do well to adopt the noble, disinterested Christian motto: "If meat make my brother to offend, I will eat no flesh while the world standeth;" or if the theatre, or dancing, or tobacco, or the wine-cup, or cards, or any minor evil, lessen my influence as a Christian teacher, I will cheerfully abandon them at once and for ever. "Be ye holy in all manner of conversation and godliness."

Examples of Teaching.

In appending some examples or lessons in teaching, I have selected two varieties from the "Gall" or "Lesson System," of which the late James Gall, of Edinburgh, was the author. I have done so, first, because it is a *system* and conforms to all good rules of teaching; secondly, because, having used it for more than a quarter of a century, I have found it to be of more value to the teacher and interest to the children than any or all others, if varied and *adapted* with a sound discretion; and, thirdly, because there are more suggestions in it to teachers than any other; in fact, it includes all others. Particular care must be taken not to attempt too much. Never attempt to use the whole *ten* exercises on any *one* Sabbath lesson, or pursue the same order. Generally use the catechetical, the explanations, and the lesson every Sabbath. In some lessons five or six can be used. All are suggestive.

The great leading principle of the system is to teach *the use of knowledge*—not to communicate information merely, but to train the young, by certain definite rules, to *make use* of all the information they receive. The first lesson here given is for younger classes; the second for more advanced:

Lesson No. 1.

As taught by the "Gall Lesson System."

(Matt. viii. 1-3.)

"When he was come down from the *mountain*, great *multitudes followed* him. And *behold*, there came a *leper* and *worshipped* him, saying, Lord, if thou *wilt* thou *canst* make me *clean*. And Jesus *put forth* his hand, and *touched* him, saying, I will; be thou *clean*. And *immediately* his *leprosy* was *cleansed*."

Who came down from the mountain? From what did Jesus come down? What happened when Jesus came down from the mountain? Who followed him? Whom did the multitudes follow?

Who came to Jesus? To whom did the leper come? What did the leper do when he came to Jesus? Whom did the leper worship? When did the leper worship Jesus? What did the leper call Jesus? Whom did the leper call Lord? What did the leper say? If who would? What could Jesus do if he would? What did the leper say Jesus could do? Who could make him clean?

What did Jesus do? Who put forth his hand? What did Jesus put forth? What did Jesus do when he put forth his hand? Who touched him? Whom did Jesus touch? When did Jesus touch the leper? What did Jesus say? Who would? What was the leper to be? Who said he was to be clean?

What happened when Jesus said he was to be clean? What was cleansed? Whose leprosy was cleansed? When was the man's leprosy cleansed? By whom was the man's leprosy cleansed?

How many circumstances are mentioned in this passage? (Nine.) What is the first? (*Multitudes followed Jesus when he came down from the mountain.*) What does that teach you? *Lesson.*—We should follow Jesus, and take every opportunity of receiving his instructions.

What is the second circumstance here mentioned? (*A leper came to Jesus to be healed of his leprosy.*) What does that teach you? *Lesson.*—We should apply to Jesus the Saviour to be healed of the leprosy of sin.

What is the third circumstance mentioned in this passage? (*The leper worshipped Jesus.*) What does that teach you? *Lesson.*—We should worship the Lord Jesus Christ as the Son of God and our only Saviour.

What is the fourth circumstance here mentioned? (*The leper doubted the willingness of Christ to cure him.*) What does that teach you? *Lesson.*—We should never doubt the willingness of Christ to do us good and to save our souls.

What is the fifth circumstance mentioned in this passage? (*The leper expressed his faith in Christ's ability to cure him.*) What does that teach you? *Lesson.*—We should cherish in our hearts a firm belief of Christ's ability to save us to the uttermost.

What is the sixth circumstance mentioned in this passage? (*Jesus put forth his hand and only touched him.*) What does that teach you? *Lesson.*—Jesus is able to save us either by the use of means or without them.

What is the seventh circumstance mentioned in this passage? (*Jesus assured the leper of his willingness.*) What does that teach you? *Lesson.*—We should assure doubting inquirers of Christ's willingness as well as ability to save them.

What is the eighth circumstance mentioned in this passage? (*Jesus immediately commanded a cure.*) *Lesson.*—None will ever seriously apply to Jesus in vain.

What is the ninth circumstance mentioned in this passage? (*The leprosy was immediately cleansed.*) What does that teach you? *Lesson.*—God is able instantly to cure the most inveterate diseases of both body and soul.

Explanation of Words to precede the Lessons.

Mountain,—High hill. *Multitudes*,—Number of people. *Followed*,—Went after. *Behold*,—Take notice. *Leper*,—Man troubled with the disease called leprosy. *Worshipped*,—Paid divine honors to. *Wilt*,—Pleaseth. *Canst*,—Art able to. *Clean*,—Free from this disease. *Put forth*,—Stretched out. *Touched*,—Laid it upon. *Clean*,—Healed. *Immediately*,—At the very instant. *Leprosy*,—Disease. *Cleansed*,—Healed or cured.

Lesson No. 2.

As taught by the "Gall Lesson System."

NOTE.—Only a part of the *ten* exercises given are to be used in any one lesson.

Question. What does God require of all those who will be saved?

Answer. God *requires* from those who will be *saved*, true *faith* in his Son Jesus *Christ;* true *repentance* of *all* their sins; and *a new* and *sincere obedience to* all his *commandments*, *from* love to *Him* who *first loved us.*

1. *Verbal and General Exercise.*

What does God require from those who will be saved? Who requires true faith? From whom does God require true faith? Who will be what?

What kind of faith does God require?

In whom are we to have true faith? Who is Jesus Christ? Whose Son is Jesus Christ? Who is the Son of God?

What does God require besides true faith? What kind of repentance does God require? From whom does God require true repentance?

Of what are they to repent? Of how many of their sins must they repent?

What does God require besides faith and repentance? From whom does God require new and sincere obedience?

What kind of obedience does God require? What is it to be new and sincere? To what does God require obedience? To whose commandments are we to give obedience? How many of God's commandments are we to obey?

From what are we to obey God's commandments? Whom are we to love? What are we to do from love to God? What did God do to us? Whom did God love? Who loved us? When did God love us?

2. *Numerical Exercise.*

How many things does God require from those who will be saved? (*Three.*—1. Faith. 2. Repentance. 3. Obedience.) What is the first? etc.

How many things are here stated with respect to faith? (*Two.*—1. It is to be a true faith. 2. It is to be faith in Jesus Christ.)

How many things are here stated with respect to repentance? (*Two.*—1. It is to be a true repentance. 2. It is to be a universal repentance.) What is the first? etc.

How many things are here stated with respect to obedience? (*Four.*—1. It is to be a new obedience. 2. A sincere obedience. 3. It is to be a universal obedience. 4. It is to be an obedience founded upon, and flowing from, love.) What is the first? etc.

3. *Doctrines Separated.*

How many doctrines are contained in this answer? (*Four.*—1. God requires true faith from all who will be saved. 2. God requires true repentance. 3. God requires a new and sincere obedience. 4. God requires us to obey all his commandments from a principle of love.) What is the first? etc.

4. *Explanations and Illustrations.*

Requires, asks, or demands. *Saved*, delivered from the power and consequences of sin. *Faith*, belief, and assured confidence. *Christ*, the anointed Saviour. *Repentance*, sorrow for, and hatred of, sin. *All*, the whole of. *A new*, not the former, but a better. *Sincere*, a pure, simple, and honest. *Obedience to*, submission to, and ready compliance with. *Commandments*, wishes, and orders. *From*, arising out of. *Him*, God. *First loved us*, had previously showed his love to us by sending his Son to die for us.

5. *Doctrines Proved.*

(1.) *God requires true faith from all who will be saved.—Mark* xvi. 16. He that believeth, and is baptized, shall be saved; but he that believeth not shall be damned.

(2.) *God requires true repentance.—Luke* xiii. 3. Except ye repent, ye shall all likewise perish.

(3.) *God requires new and sincere obedience.—Rom.* vi. 17. But ye have obeyed from the heart that form of doctrine which was delivered you.

(4.) *God requires us to obey all his commandments from a principle of love.—John* xiv. 15. If ye love me, keep my commandments.

6. *Lessons from the Doctrines.*

From these doctrines we learn,

(1.) That we should beware of unbelief.

(2.) That we should hate and forsake sin.
(3.) That our obedience to God should be cheerful and constant.
(4.) That all our duties should be done to please God rather than ourselves.

7. *Application of the Lessons.*

Of what should we beware? (1.)
What should we hate and forsake? (2.)
What should be cheerful and constant? (3.)
Whom should we seek to please in the performance of duty? (4.)

8. *Devotional Exercise (from the Answer.)*

Petition.—Bestow upon us, we beseech thee, those graces which thou requirest from all those who will be saved. Give to each of us true faith in thy Son Jesus Christ, true repentance of all our sins, and a new and sincere obedience to all thy commandments, arising from love to thee who hast first loved us.

9. *Devotional Exercise (from the Lessons.)*

O Lord, may we always be upon our guard, (1.) and constantly beware of falling into the sin of unbelief. May we sincerely repent of all our transgressions, (2.) and heartily hate and forsake all sin. And grant that (3.) our obedience to thee may be cheerful and constant; and that (4.) all our duties may be done to honor and obey thee, rather than to please ourselves.

10. *Paraphrase formed.*

God [asks or demands] *from those who will be* [delivered from the power and consequences of sin,] *true* [belief and assured confidence] *in his Son Jesus,* [the anointed Saviour,] *true* [sorrow for, and hatred] *of,* [the whole of] *their sins, and* [not the former, but a better] *and* [a pure, simple, and honest] submission to and ready compliance with] *all his* [wishes and orders,] [arising out of, and proceeding from,] *love to* [God,] *who* [had previously showed his love to us, by sending his Son to die for us.]

Other Modes of Teaching.

There are also various other modes of teaching that can be used on different lessons. One plan is to raise the questions Who? What? When? and Where?

Another is to take the letters P. P. D. D. D. D.,

the two P's and four D's, and inquire for *P-ersons*, *P-laces*, *D-ates*, *D-oings*, *D-octrines*, and *D-uties*.

Another still is to take the word "*F-i-d-d-l-e-r*," as a mnemonic for the teacher's use. The first letter, *F*, will remind him to call on the children to tell him what *facts*, and how many, are to be found in the first verse or in the lesson. The next letter, *i*, may prompt him to call for *inferences* or *instructions*. The letter *d* repeated would remind him to ask for the *doctrines* and *duties*, *l* will call for *lessons*, *e* for *examples*, and *r* for *rebukes*. This will give active employment to the children—a thing which they delight in, and it will aid the teacher in the difficult but sublime work of teaching divine Truth.

XI.

ILLUSTRATIVE TEACHING.

O illustrate is to throw light upon, to illumine, to make clear and plain. Illustration has, also, a decorating power as well as an enlightening power.

Illustrative teaching is not merely entertaining or amusing the children with stories and anecdotes, but may comprise them incidentally. Explanation appeals to the understanding, while illustration appeals to the observation of the young. Says one writer: "It is by illustration alone, which appeals to their observation, that ideas are conveyed to children's minds." Anecdotes and stories are generally too long for Sunday-school teaching, and the danger is that they will overshadow the truth. Illustrative teaching should be employed in the Sabbath-school to make divine truth glow and become plainer, clearer, and better understood—nothing else. It must never displace the lesson, but be held in strict subordination to it. Illustrations of divine truths are very useful—in fact, indispensable; but dangerous, unless well guarded so as never to withdraw attention from the Bible.

This was one of our divine Saviour's chosen modes of teaching, as we see in the beautiful parable of the sower, and, in fact, in almost all of His inimitable parables. Mankind, as well as children, delight in this form of instruction. Says Mr. Groser, in his excellent work on this subject: "Children have a passion for details and revel in analogies. Mark their fondness for *stories*, however frivolous; *word-pictures*, however meagre, and *comparisons*, however commonplace." Tupper says:

"Principles and rules are repulsive to a child, but happy illustration winneth him.
In vain shalt thou preach of industry and prudence till he learn of the bee and ant.
Dimly will he think of his soul, till the acorn and the chrysalis have taught him.
He will fear God in thunder, and worship His loveliness in flowers.
And parables shall charm his heart, while doctrines seem dead mystery."

Illustration is something laid alongside of—parallel—for comparison, and should be short, obvious, and appropriate. There must always be something to illustrate.

For instance: If we were teaching, "Take us the foxes, the little foxes," etc., we could illustrate the danger and influence of little evils or sins by saying: Chemists tell us that a single grain of iodine will color

7000 times its weight in water; so a little sin may discolor and destroy a good character. A ruined man once said: "It was that ten minutes on the street-corner, reading a bad book, that destroyed my whole life." "It was that penny I stole when a very young boy," said an old man, "that sent me four times to prison, and confined me twenty-eight years out of sixty of my life, and all for stealing less than thirty-eight dollars."

Or if the lesson was, "No man can serve two masters," etc., let the teacher say: "The other day I saw two men together walking down the avenue, and a little dog was running behind them; so they went on for a while, and I wondered to which of them the dog belonged. When they came to the corner of a certain street they shook hands and went opposite ways. Then I saw at once to which of them the little dog belonged. He could not follow both; so he trotted after his master. So, dear children, it is with you; you may try to be Christ's servants and the servants of Satan at the same time, but it will be in vain; 'You cannot serve God and mammon.'"

If on the subject of falsehood, we would impress our pupils with the fact that the degree does not affect criminality. An apt illustration will be found in "Eve and the forbidden fruit."

The Bible is full of perfect examples, if rightly selected. "Old Humphrey," the English writer for children, abounded in pertinent illustrations. I copy

8 *

one: "Think not that because you look like other teachers or scholars, and undertake the same duties, that no difference is seen by those around you. You may look alike and be altogether different."

Illustration 1. "I came to two frozen ponds, so much alike in size and form that at the first view one might have been regarded as the counterpart of the other. This was, however, very far from being the case; for, after making a hole in the ice, I found one to be only a few inches deep, while with my stick I could not reach the bottom of the other."

2. "I picked up two walnuts as they lay among the dry leaves, under the tree on which they had grown; both were large, and I thought that each would be good; but, no! one was altogether hollow, while the other contained a capital kernel."

3. "I bought two apples at a fruit-stand—ruddy and ripe; I do not believe the man who sold them to me could have pointed out any difference between them; and yet, for all this, when I came to turn them around and examine them, I found one of them to be firm and sound, and the other rotten to the very core."

"As it was with the ponds, the walnuts, and the apples, so it may be with you. Some are shallow, while others have depth of understanding; some have depth of understanding, while others are shallow; some are full of knowledge, while others are empty; and some are firm and to be relied upon, while others are unsound at their hearts."

These are short and very simple, but excellent and to the point.

The Bible is full of perfect examples of illustrative teaching. The parables are mostly of this order. The parable of the sower, with the field and husbandman before him, as is probable, is a striking example of illustrative teaching. In the gospels, how constantly our Saviour began His parables with, "The kingdom of heaven is *likened* unto," or is "*like*," etc. Said an old divine to a young preacher: "I see you do not follow Christ's example in your preaching; for you have no '*likes*' in your sermons." Do we *liken* Bible truth to something with which our scholars are familiar, and thus help them to understand it?

Illustrations abound all around us. Some years ago there was published a work entitled "Spiritual Honey from Natural Hives." I do not know but it is now out of print; but it contained no less than 258 illustrations of various passages of Scripture—all drawn from the honey-bee, and most of them were valuable. For example: "Mercy comes naturally from God, like honey from the bee; but justice, like the sting, only when she is provoked." "If nature teaches the bee not only to gather honey out of sweet flowers, but out of bitter, shall not grace teach us to draw, even out of the bitterest condition, something to better our souls?" "Many hate not sin, nor fly from it, because it is *sin;* but as children do bees; not because they are bees, but because they have a *sting*. So do these persons flee from sin; not because it is *sinful*, but because it is *hurtful*."

The following convey important lessons to Bible-students: "If you do but take and pierce God's word, and do but stay upon it, as the bee doth on the flower, and *will not off* till you have got something out of it; if you still be digging in this mine, this will make you rich in knowledge; and if you be rich in knowledge, it will make you rich in grace." Finally: "Some use flowers only for the beauty or the smell; the physicians, for health; the bees, for honey; so do wise and prudent persons apply their studies for the enriching and feeding of their minds."

The late eloquent Rev. Dr. Payson was accustomed to illustrate under the form of apt *suppositions*. For instance, said he: "Suppose you wished to separate a quantity of brass and steel filings mixed together in one vessel; how would you effect this separation? Apply a loadstone, and immediately every particle of iron will attach itself to it, while the brass filings remain behind. Thus, if we see a company of true and false professors of religion, we may not be able to distinguish them; but let Christ come among them, and all His sincere followers will be attracted towards Him, as the steel is drawn to the magnet, while those who have none of His spirit will remain at a distance." Again: On a visit to a weeping mother, who refused to be comforted for the loss of a beloved child: "Suppose, now," said he, "some one was making a beautiful crown for you to wear, and that you knew it was for you, and that you were to receive it and wear it as soon as it should be done; now, if the maker of it were to come, and in order to make the crown more beautiful and splendid, were to take some of your jewels to put into it, should you be sorrowful and unhappy because they were taken away for a little while, when you knew they were going to make up your crown? He can take better care of them than you could." The mother smiled through her tears at the thought that her jewel was taken from her but for a season, and said, in meek submission: "The Lord gave, and the Lord hath taken away; blessed be the name of the Lord."

The question here arises, From whence shall Sunday-school teachers gather illustrations for use? I reply, generally, everywhere, and from everything; but to particularize: 1. From the home-surroundings, circumstances, and home-life of the pupils. 2. Facts and incidents that are constantly occurring around us. "*Facts* are the arguments of God," said Rev. Dr. Chalmers. 3. History, biography, and geography—sacred and profane. 4. Agriculture, horticulture, and botany. 5. Proverbs, maxims, wise sayings, and poetry. 6. Emblems, similes, metaphors, etc. 7. Science and art; manners and customs.

I need not extend this list, for these will readily suggest many others to the teacher.

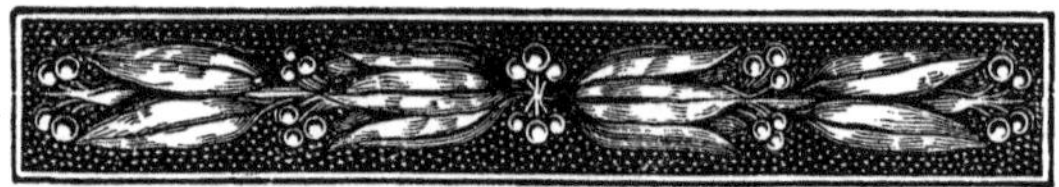

XII.

PICTORIAL TEACHING.

ICTORIAL teaching is only a slightly different form of Bible illustration, and, therefore, will appropriately follow the previous subject.

It presents, first, pictures and maps to the pupils for examination, in order that they may get a clearer view of truth. It consists, secondly, more particularly in picturing out in words, or in vivid, graphic description, so that the truth will appear real to the imagination of the child. It awakens interest and deepens impression, and all good teachers avail themselves, more or less, of its power.

"But," says a quiet teacher, "all this must be graphically done." I reply: "Of course it must;" and the answer returns: "Well, I can't use it, then, for I am not graphic." I will give all such teachers a recipe that will render them always graphic with children. If they would dwell clearly and plainly on all the little details in their descriptions to children, they will always be graphic. The imaginations of scholars of ten or twelve years of age are so vivid that much of the teacher's power over them, to interest and impress truth, will depend largely upon this power of "word-picturing." Words containing objects largely should be most used, instead of a mass of sentiments and principles. Let the objective words preponderate.

The following statement embraces about a dozen words in *principles:*

"It was David's *duty* to *know* the *will* of God, and as he had great *faith* in the divine *power*, he went forth without *reluctance* to meet the *foe*, and the *result* was the death of Goliath."

Let us now transpose the sentence into *objects* mainly, and it will not be difficult to see which will make the clearest and best impression upon children's minds:

"Young David *stood* in the *valley* and slung a *stone* into the *forehead* of the *giant*, Goliath, and he *fell* dead upon the ground."

Abbott gives many illustrations. He says:

"You tell a man, 'He went down to the shore, and got into a boat and pushed off.' You would interest a child more if you say, 'He went down to the shore and found a boat there. One end of the boat—the front part, which they call the bow—was up against the shore, a little in the sand. The other end was out of the water, and moved up and down gently with the waves. There were seats across the boat, and two oars lying upon the seats. The man stepped upon the bow of the boat; it was fast in the mud.'

And so on, describing the water under one end, and sand under the other; the one end rocking and rattling the oars, and th. man walking back and pushing the boat off," etc.

Be exceedingly minute, therefore, with little children. In all the details which you describe take very short steps, and take each one distinctly. The Bible narratives are wonderfully adapted to good pictorial teaching. Bible emblems, which so abound, must be carefully pictured out; as, "The Lord God is a sun and shield," a "rock," and "refuge." "As the hart panteth," etc. Detail it so as to make the scene as real as possible to the child, and enable him to see the hart, the mountain, the water brooks, etc. Suppose you were on the lesson of the apprehension and trial of Christ:

"Children, see that crowd of people wending their way through the streets of Jerusalem! Some of them carry torches or lanterns in their hands; others have staves or swords. See, in the midst of them there walks one who looks very kind, but very sorrowful. Who is it? It is Jesus. The multitude, led on by the cruel priests, have just been to the garden of Gethsemane and hurried him away from His disciples; and now they are going to take Him before their rulers, that they may have Him put to death. Then describe the High Priest, Pilate, and Herod; the judgment hall, the drops of blood, the soldiers, and crown of thorns; the cross, the angry cries of, "Crucify Him!"

All this must be done with care and exactness, and before adopting it the teacher must make himself *very familiar* with every part, so as never to hesitate or labor in it; and then afterward call it all back by questions, in the children's own language.

Again: Suppose you wished to make a lasting impression on a child while developing a single important thought; as, for instance, the omniscience of God. Talk candidly to the child somewhat as follows:

"Mary, do you know that God knows all things? He saw Adam and Eve when they hid themselves in the trees of the garden. He saw Moses when he lay in his little ark by the side of the river. He saw Timothy when his mother taught him to read the Bible. He sees every person in the world just now. You know in Africa there are a great many millions of men and women. They are black. They are called negroes. God sees them all, and he sees the missionaries who are there teaching them God's word; and at the very same moment he sees all the people of this country, and every person in this town. He sees you, Mary. He saw you when you were a little babe in your cradle; he sees you at all your plays, and in the school; he knows what you say, and what you think; he sees every tear that falls from your eye, and every smile that plays on your cheek; he hears you sing his praises; and when you pray, Mary, God listens to everything that you ask; and when you lie down, and the room is dark and still, and there is nothing moving but your pulse, and nothing heard but your breathing, then God sees you, for the darkness and the light are both alike to Him."

Thus dwell *amply* on a thought until you associate it in the child's mind with many circumstances. For Bible-classes, of course, a teacher would not descend to all the details of some of these examples, yet in every age and class be graphic and life-like in word-picturing. The parables of the prodigal son, and of the good Samaritan, are divinely beautiful examples of pictorial teaching, for when our Saviour wanted to impress love to our neighbor he *pictured* out for us the beautiful story of the good Samaritan.

The following example is from "David Stow's Bible-training," published in Edinburgh, and is the "Training System" pictured out in words:

Example.

"As the hart panteth after the water brooks, so panteth my soul after thee, O God." Ps. xlii. 1. The more common way that the pious teacher or parent takes, is to pass over the emblem, and at once proceed with the spiritual lesson—*thus beginning at the end*—without any natural picture having been presented to the mind's eye of the pupils, by which they may be assisted to the analogy—*as* and *so*, as the Natural, so the Spiritual—which is so uniformly done by the Spirit of God in Scripture.

Points in the Natural Picture to be brought out.

1. Some points in the natural history of the hart—different names given to the animal—swiftness of foot—where generally lives. 2. Frequently hunted. 3. Where to flee to in a mountainous country, as Judea, when pursued—hills or valleys. 4. Heat, drought, dust—effect on the animal, particularly after running—thirst. 5. Running about seeking for water—increasing—not merely a drink, but a brook, where it may plunge in as well as drink. 6. Why, then, a brook, and not a stream?—picture out a brook. 7. Brooks more likely to be found in plains—but animal pursued there. 8. The hart, heated and thirsty, therefore *pants*—

what is panting? 9. Has the hart ever bathed in water brooks before? If not, would it have panted and longed for it? The full picturing out of these points (even in the incomplete and imperfect manner that can be done on paper) would greatly exceed our limits. The natural picture or condition of the hart being visible to the minds of the children, the analogy to the circumstances in which David was placed will appear, viz., pursued by his enemies, and especially by his own son, Absalom—fleeing to the mountains for safety —away from the sanctuary, etc., etc. He, no doubt, on seeing the harts near him panting and seeking for water brooks, mournfully and longingly expressed himself: "So panteth my soul after thee, O God."

TEACHER.—I must tell you, children, before we commence our lesson, that it is supposed this psalm was written by David, who was obliged to flee from his enemies to the land of Jordan, and that when there he probably took up his abode in the mountains, away from the public worship of . . . *God's house*, and seeing the harts running . . . Where? *about the hills*, and panting for thirst, most likely induced him to use the . : . What metaphor or emblem did he use? Look at your books. David says: "As the hart panteth after the. . . . *water-brooks* (read on, children), *so panteth my soul after thee, O God.*"

The first thing we must speak about in this picture is the . . . *hart*. What is a hart? Can you tell me any other names given to the hart? *Stag—deer—gazelle—roe.* Very right; these are the names given to . . . *this animal*, or . . . *species.*

Well, the name of this animal or . . . *species*, is called . . . the *hart*. Is it a slow or quick moving animal? *Swift.* It runs . . . *very swiftly.* What countries do harts chiefly live in? *Mountainous countries.* Why do you think so? *The Bible says, "Like a young roe upon the mountains."* And a young roe is . . . *a young hart.* Well, that is one proof that they live in the mountains; but can they live in the plains? *Yes, sir; they live in plains in gentlemen's parks*, which are sometimes . . . *plain*, or nearly . . . *level*. Very well; but when allowed to roam and run about freely and . . . *naturally*, they . . . *prefer the mountains*. Is the hart spoken of in the psalm supposed to live in a warm or cold country, think you? *A warm country*. Why? . . . Bring down the map, children, and show the country or countries you suppose to be meant. (The map of Palestine is presented.) Point out those parts you think harts live in. You think the Psalmist means . . . *the mountainous parts of Palestine*. And Palestine is . . . What sort of a country? *Mountainous country*, and . . . *very hot*. Now, we must get smartly on. The hart lives in . . . *a hot country*, and in the mountainous parts of . . . *a hot country*. How does the sun shine? *Over head, nearly perpendicular*, and, therefore, the great part of the year the ground must be . . . *very hot and dry*. In what state will the soil be? *Parched and dusty*. And in mountainous countries, where the sun is very hot, what happens to the streams or brooks? *The brooks dry up*. It is then a dry and . . . *thirsty land*, and where . . . *no water is*. If you turn in your Bible to Job vi. 15, it is said: "And as the stream of brooks they pass away,"—showing that the brooks in that hot climate are . . . *very apt to pass away*, or . . . *dry up*.

Tell me, children, what you mean by panting? Show me what panting is? This boy thinks it is simply opening the mouth. (Take nothing for granted.) Have you ever seen a dog walking in a very hot and dusty day, after having run a long way? *Yes, sir; it opens its mouth*. Does it simply open its mouth, as this boy did? *It pants, this way. It feels uneasy*. Why uneasy? *Because it is weary and thirsty*. Weary and thirsty from . . . *the heat;* and a thirsty dog, that is weary and very . . . *hot*, would—what would it wish? *To have a drink*, or, perhaps, to . . . *plunge in the brook*.

Of what had the hart drank before? *The brooks.* Well, the hart having both drank of . . . *the brook*, and . . . *plunged in the brook before*, longed and . . . *panted to do so again.* In this sad condition, therefore—heated and . . . *thirsty*, and running about, . . . *panting*—how would the hart feel? Would he be satisfied to lie down? *No, sir; very anxious.* And what more? *Longing and panting for water.* Not at rest, because it . . . *felt*—the . . . *want of something* it could not get at . . . *that time;* and that was . . *the water brooks.*

Now, let us look at the verse, and see in what state or . . . *condition* the hart is supposed to be. Repeat it, if you please, each word, separately, slowly, and distinctly. "As, the, hart, panteth, after, the, water, brooks." What is a brook? *A clear stream*—not a muddy, stagnant . . . *pool.* Do you think the hart had drank of a brook before? *Yes; else it would not have panted for it.* What makes the hart so very thirsty? *Because it runs about the hills, where there is no water.* And as the hart opens . . . *its mouth*, and . . . *pants for water*, and runs about, it raises the . . . What do you think it raises? *The dust into its mouth.* And what does the dust do? *Increases its thirst*, and causes the hart to long more for . . . *the brooks*—which are now . . . *dried up*—or, perhaps, at a . . . *great distance.* What would you expect the hart to do were it to reach a brook? *Drink plentifully*—and, also, . . . *plunge into the water.* Why? *To cool* and . . . *refresh itself.* The application, or spiritual lesson, is by recalling the *hart*, on the *mountains*, *hunted by dogs*, *shot at by arrows*, *hot and thirsty*, *panting* for *water brooks*, for a *plunge-bath*, and *drink.* So, David fleeing on the mountains for life, pursued by enemies, *longing* for safety, and for the public worship of God at Jerusalem, *panting* for the Lord's house, where *God's law* was read, and the true God was worshipped, etc. He *desired*, *longed* for, *panted*, *prayed* for God, the living God.

Children, do *you so long for*, and *pant after* God, the living God? etc., etc.

Another form of pictorial teaching is, after questioning the lesson out of the scholars, and then in again, and explaining all the words, etc., to paint imaginary pictures of the events described in the lesson. Thus, in a lesson from Matt. xiv. 22–33, taught by the Rev. Edward Eggleston, of Chicago, he said to the first pupil: "Carrie, suppose that you were a painter with your canvas before you, what picture would you draw from the 22d verse?" She replied, "Christ sending his disciples and the multitudes away." "Mary, what from the 23d verse?" "Christ on the mountain, alone, in prayer." "Jane, what from the 24th verse?" "The ship tossed with the waves." "Lily, what from verse 25?" "Jesus walking on the sea." The next, "Peter sinking, Jesus saving;" and then, "The sea calm, all safe in the ship, worshipping Jesus." From these the lessons drawn are "Secret prayer," "Looking to Jesus for help in danger," "Not seeking danger," and that "Jesus is God," to control the wind and waves. The doctrine is the Divinity of Christ: "Of a truth, thou art the Son of God."

"Pictorial Teaching," by Hartley and Groser, on Illustrative Teaching, further illustrates these subjects.

XIII.

OBJECT-TEACHING.

HIS is presenting an object to look at, for the purpose of getting a clearer and more perfect view of the truth taught. It is simply calling to our aid the *eye*. The eye is one of our two great learning senses. It has been called "the king of the senses," and it is emphatically so with children; for little children learn the most that they do learn through the eye. Bunyan quaintly says: "Come to the mind and soul through Eye-gate as well as through Ear-gate." This is the most pleasant and effective way of giving and receiving some kinds of knowledge. It cultivates, also, the important habit of close and accurate observation. Says the Rev. Dr. Hill, the President of Harvard University: "It is the thought of God in the object that stimulates the child's thought." The great object is to teach the child more than you can express in words. In illustration, he says: "I was walking yesterday with my little girl, and showing her plants, insects, and birds as we walked along. We were looking at lichens on the trees, when she suddenly, and without

hint from me, said: 'The maples have different lichens from the ash. I mean to see if I can tell trees by their trunks, without looking at their leaves.' So for a long distance she kept her eyes down, saying to the trees as she passed: 'Elm, maple, ash, pine,' etc.—never failing. The difference was easy to *see*, but the difference could not have been so well expressed in *words*."

Our schools of public instruction are largely using this mode of teaching in the early years of school-life, with great gratification to the children, and, also, with great success. The size, form, shape, color, origin, and uses of many articles are thus taught, incidentally weaving in spelling, reading, and a vast amount of useful knowledge. If this were all, however, it would hardly avail much in our Sabbath-schools above the infant class. But we apprehend that in some particular Sabbath-school lessons, but not in all, object-teaching can be used to great advantage by all classes and conditions of scholars. Never force or crowd object-teaching, however, upon any lesson.

The simple difference between object-teaching and illustrative teaching is this: If you were teaching on the words "Though your sins be red like crimson, they shall be as wool," in *illustrative* teaching, we should tell the children that the Turkey-red dyes are so firm that no bleacher's salts will make them white, and therefore, we make the Turkey-red rags into pink blotting-paper; in *object*-teaching, we hold up the Turkey-red calico, explain it, and then *show* the pink blotting-paper—making it, by help of the two objects and the explanation, more impressive with children. In fact, there are lessons that cannot be plainly taught without the use of objects. They need, however, to be used with discretion; and upon Bible lessons only on those that will make the truths *better* understood.

We have, however, the highest authority for the use of objects in teaching religious truths. Our Saviour himself practised this mode of teaching. It will be remembered that when the crafty Scribes and Pharisees sought to entangle him in his talk, and proposed the question—"Master, is it lawful to give tribute unto Cæsar or not?" he, perceiving their wickedness, said: "Why tempt ye me, ye hypocrites? Show me the tribute-money. And they brought unto Him a penny." Why did the divine Redeemer, who never did a superfluous thing, or spoke a superfluous word,—why did He, who is infinite in wisdom, call for this penny? We may safely reply, Because it was divinely *best* and needful. He wanted to bring to bear the two great learning senses, to wit, *seeing* and *hearing*. He then directed the eyes of these scheming men to the coin, with this pointed question: "Whose is this image and superscription? They said unto him, Cæsar's." Then came the inimitable *application* of the lesson —without which every lesson is a failure—viz.: "Render therefore unto Cæsar the things which be

Cæsar's, and unto God the things which be God's." We are told that "when they had heard these words, they marvelled, and left him, and went their way." The lesson was conclusive.

At another time, you remember that our Saviour "called a little child unto him and set him in the midst of them," to teach his disciples the answer to their query, "Who is the greatest in the kingdom of heaven?" Here the little child was the object. The lesson is obvious to all. Even in the memorial service of our Saviour's death, he called for two *objects*—the bread and the wine. It was divinely necessary.

We may seem almost to see the same divine Teacher bending forward and pointing his disciples to the beautiful flowers at his feet, exclaiming: "Behold the lilies of the field," or look at the "fowls of the air," or see "the fields white unto the harvest," or the falling sparrow, or the fig-tree, and a multitude of similar objects all around them, which were used by him in his wonderful teaching, and with such success that they were led to exclaim: "Never man spake like this man." The whole of the types and ceremonies in the Old Testament were but a magnificent series of this mode of object-teaching. This is the whole, in substance, of object-teaching. It is Christ's mode and the prophet's way of teaching. "It is nature's teaching," says a teacher at our side. There is *no* teaching, scarcely, that is not, in some sense, object-teaching. Said the Rev. Dr. Chester, when describing good teaching: "This is object-teaching, as all good teaching of the young is. You must take their measure if you would fit the garment of truth to them." Objects for teaching lie all over nature as clearly as in cubes and squares and octagons. It keeps each child pleasantly and profitably employed. It is calling the eye and senses to our aid in affecting the mind and heart. The eye is our first teacher. Hence it is indispensably necessary in an infant class to have plenty of objects. Every good mother and good juvenile class-teacher will make great use of the *eye* and *action* and *motion* to teach and impress the great truths of the lesson upon the little ones. Use the eye more, and make your words few and well chosen. "Present to the children *things* before *words*, or *ideas* before *names*." Even in manners and morals let the *person*, *life* and *tongue* of the teacher be the "object." "She openeth her mouth with wisdom, and in her tongue is the law of kindness."

Here is an art that every teacher should become facile in, *i. e.*, looking up and using objects that will serve our purpose in teaching; and for this reason, he should always wear his "Sunday-school spectacles." A sprig of evergreen, or a bit of a vine picked from the bush as we pass our garden-gate for the Sunday-school, may serve to illustrate the duty of "abiding in Christ" as the branch must abide in the vine. A little flower or grass, or a falling leaf, will illustrate, through the eye, the brevity of life, and that "we all do fade as a leaf." Even a pin may be used as an object, from whence to draw lessons as to the value, use, and importance of *little things*. When the pin is crooked and rendered useless, we can with it rebuke crooked tempers or crooked tongues or characters.

A child may be led to see "the whole armor of God" in a picture of an old knight with his "helmet," "shield," "breastplate," and "sword." A plaster cast of a *faithful* dog, loving doves, little Samuel in prayer, or David with his shepherd's staff, have all been frequently used to teach divine lessons. A specimen of good fruit will teach us to bring forth good fruit—to be fruit-bearers; and the showing of a watch may be made the means of much valuable instruction to children.

But we must sum up some of the leading things which may be used in Sunday-school object-teaching, viz.:

1. Natural objects.
2. Texts, cards, etc.
3. Maps, charts, etc.
4. Pictures and drawings.
5. Word-painting, or pictorial teaching by aid of the imagination.
6. Parables, parallels, etc.
7. Portable slates and paper.
8. The blackboard, which furnishes ample facilities for object-teaching.

Object Lessons in Brief Notes.

Examples.

The following is an outline lesson on a picture-print of

David and Goliath. 1 Sam. xvii.

Ps. xviii. 32: Success is from the Lord.

First. Remarks and questions on the print. Ask the children to point out the two principal figures—to tell you what difference they observe in them; one is an immense man—a giant; the other a young lad. The difference in their dress—one is clad in armor, with helmet, shield, and spear; the other has a light dress, with a crook, a sling, and a bag. Let them describe the manner and action of each. The giant looks fierce and angry, raising his spear and clenching his enormous fist. The lad appears calm and gentle; casting his look upwards, he points to heaven. For what purpose do they seem to be met? How can the youth escape so great and powerful an enemy? Where can he look for help? Ask the children what they would do under the circumstances.

Secondly. The narrative. Give the children an account from the Bible of Goliath's size and his armor, and let them see how complete the latter was. Read to them how he defied the armies of the living God, and challenged any to combat with him. Who is able to stand against so mighty an enemy? All the Israelite soldiers are afraid. At last a slender youth comes forward and offers himself. How is he prepared for the contest? What makes him so bold? Read verses 32-37. He trusts in the Lord. It is His cause in which he fights. This is David. See how he prepares himself (verse 40). His spirit is shown in verses 45, 46.

Success was with David (see 48-50). Contrast the appearance of the two, their different preparation and their spirit.

Lesson. David fought in the name of the Lord, trusted in His strength, and sought His glory. How can we imitate him? All sin, all evil, is the enemy of the Lord: we must fight against them in His strength and seeking His glory, and He will make us more than conquerors.

Different Objects.

I. 1. Object, *a Leaf.* Children, what do I hold in my hand? *A leaf.* What can you tell me about it? One says it has *form;* others, *color, substance, length, breadth, thickness, branches* in its frame like the tree, all *different,* etc., etc. What is a leaf? *The clothing of trees.* Gen. viii. 11.

2. What does the Bible say about a leaf or leaves? Shall not wither, Ps. i. 3—be green, Jer. xvii. 8—not fade, Ezek. xlvii. 12—fadeth, Is. i. 30—sewed fig-leaves, Gen. iii. 7—cast their leaves, Is. vi. 13—fair, Dan. iv. 12, 21—nothing but leaves, Mark xi. 13—putteth forth leaves, Mark xiii. 28. Enlarge and illustrate any points.

3. See Rev. xxii. 2: And the *leaves* of the tree were for the healing of the nations.

See *bad, poisonous leaves.* Upas tree, poison-ivy, etc.

See *good leaves.*—Sassafras, balsam, wintergreen, etc.

The *leaves of the Bible* are for the healing of the nations, etc.

Corrupt *leaves* or bad books blight and destroy.

II. Object, *a Grapevine with cluster of fruit. Cut* branch will not *unite* again with the vine. *Prune* so as to produce fruit, otherwise will run to leaves. Taste of good fruit. See fruits of the Spirit, Gal. v. 22, love, joy, peace, etc. How bear such, etc.

III. Object, *a Pin.* Sharp, straight, and shining. How many for a penny? Thirty persons to make it. So little and cheap, not valued. So of common blessings—air, light, water. Feel your pulse. Not live without it. So *learn to value little things.*

See its value in need, as in storms, cold, etc. So value Bible, health, school, church, etc., while you have them.

Bend it, and it becomes *crooked,*—so crooked *tempers, tongues,* etc.

IV. A *Sprig of Evergreen,* broken off, may teach us to *abide* in Christ.

V. *Salt,* as a grand *preservative.* A *Rotten Apple,* influence and decay.

VI. *Flowers,* so beautiful and frail. A pansy may teach *humility,* a daisy, *cheerfulness,* a rose, *goodness* and *virtue,* a lily, *purity,* etc.

XIV.

THE BLACKBOARD.

WE would not undertake to conduct a Sabbath-school without a good blackboard. The great object of it is to direct, to concentrate, and to *fix* the attention, sympathies, and prayers of the whole school upon that portion of the word of God which is embodied in the great practical thought of the lesson. It is affectingly interesting to see a whole school, teachers and scholars, banishing their worldly thoughts, and raising their eyes and hearts apparently up to the great warm thought of God, as they cross the threshold of the school-room, and see, in clear, distinct letters on the blackboard, the key-note of the lesson for the day; as, "My son, give me thy heart." "Son, go work to-day in my vineyard." "The soul that sinneth, it shall die." "I will arise and go to my father." "Have faith in God." "All waiting for Jesus." "Flee from the wrath to come." "About my Father's business." "The blood of Jesus Christ his Son cleanseth us from all sin." "Founded on a rock," etc.

Blackboards have long been used in public schools

with great advantage, but have only been adopted in Sunday-schools during the last decade of years. They, however, prove to be so well adapted and useful that they are meeting with universal approval, and are fast coming into general use. We think a blackboard should be used in every Sabbath-school, on every Sabbath, by every superintendent, and on every lesson; for the dullest superintendent, in city or country, can plainly write or print one thought from the word of God on the blackboard, and thus fix the eye and concentrate the thought and heart of the otherwise careless, upon the lesson.

We have often seen the noisiest boys of the city calmed by this means into thoughtfulness and interest in the lesson. Sometimes colored crayons are used to attract as well as to impress. The names of the Deity are sometimes carefully written in crayon of one color, while wrath, sin, etc., may be put in another color, say *red*.

A map, drawn by the superintendent or pastor on the blackboard in the presence of the school, will have many times the effect that it will have, if we point to a regular map. A cross of two rough marks made by a teacher on a slip of paper, to illustrate the lesson, will interest a child more than will a jewelled cross, —it was made by teacher.

Frequently the superintendent or teacher will write down the answer, or the main word of the *answers* of the children on the blackboard, and this will interest them greatly. A teacher can use a piece of white paper to write or draw on for the scholars of a private class. A few points must be heeded—

1. Do not put any but well-digested, important words, thoughts, and objects on the blackboard.

2. Write or draw as plainly, neatly, and correctly as possible. Do not write too much.

3. Let all the exercises of the school bear directly towards the one great thought of the lesson.

Thus let the freshest and most prominent object in the school-room aid the teacher and superintendent, through the use of the eye, in their great work.

A word of caution is needed, however, concerning the use of the blackboard. Sometimes it has been made to appear quite ridiculous by a fanciful and perverted use of it. The only justifiable use of the blackboard in a Sabbath-school is in order to make Bible truths more clear and attractive in the eyes of teachers and scholars. Men of good taste, as well as those having tact and ingenuity, can and do use the blackboard with power in various ways. For instance, some years ago I saw a lesson taught in Ralph Wells's school—and many of my examples originated with him—from the text in Matt. v. 16: "Let your light so shine," etc. This was plainly written on the board, while on one side was drawn a figure of a light-house, with the rays of light shining forth from the lamp. The superintendent in a review pressed the question, "*How* are we to let our light shine, according to the lesson, 'So shine?'"

—and very soon the children said they were to let their light shine by "being pure," "meek," "merciful," etc., and soon the beatitudes were each written on the separate rays from the light-house lamp.

At another time I noticed the text, "Founded on a rock," together with the figure of a house firm on a rock, and another house crumbling and falling down "on the sand." See to the foundation.

A catechism lesson on the question, "What is sin?" was placed on the board "*My sin.*"

Examples of Blackboard Exercises.

The following examples are given as suggestive of several different lines of use to which the blackboard may be put:

The substance of a lesson in the 6th chapter of Matthew was once put upon the board in two words, "Outside" and "Inside," the children being asked to examine the chapter and tell what to write on the blackboard; at the end of the address the board appeared as follows, each specification having been vividly illustrated by an incident:

Outside.	*Inside.*
Alms.	Alms.
Prayer.	Prayer.
Fasting.	Fasting.
Treasures.	Treasures.

Another good lesson on the board is to take one of the commandments, for instance, the "Third Commandment." Raise three questions and get the children to fill out the answers as follows:

The Third Commandment.

How broken.	*Why broken.*	*Why not.*
Swearing.	Get mad.	'Tain't right.
Oh gracious!	Don't think.	No use.
Make fun of the Bible.	Think it's big.	Bible says we mustn't.
Praying careless.	Careless.	Mean.
Singing and not thinking.	Wicked.	Ungentlemanly.

The following lesson has been successfully given by the Rev. Mr. Ostrander, of Albany:

THOU
shalt
call
His
name

BELIEVE on The Lord JESUS Christ and thou shalt be SAVED.

for He
shall
save
His
people
from
their
SINS.

Where ought Jesus to be? *Ans.* In the heart.

Where did he get his name? *Ans.* From the angel. (Matt. i. 21.)

Why was this name given? *Ans.* (Matt. i. 22.)

How does he save from sin? *Ans.* "Believe on the Lord Jesus Christ."

Other points of instruction and application may be derived from the careful study of the above arrangement.

The following, by E. D. Jones, of St. Louis, teaches a lesson from the text, John xii. 32: "And I, if I be lifted up from the earth, will draw all men unto me." *First*, Notice the influences God uses to draw men: 1. The Holy Spirit. 2. The Bible. 3. The Churches. *Secondly*, Look at their relations: 1. As a Helper. 2. As a Teacher. 3. As a Trainer. *Thirdly*, Look at the chief work of these agents: 1. To Reveal. 2. To Believe. 3. To Know. 4. To Train. At the close of the address or lesson the blackboard will appear as follows:

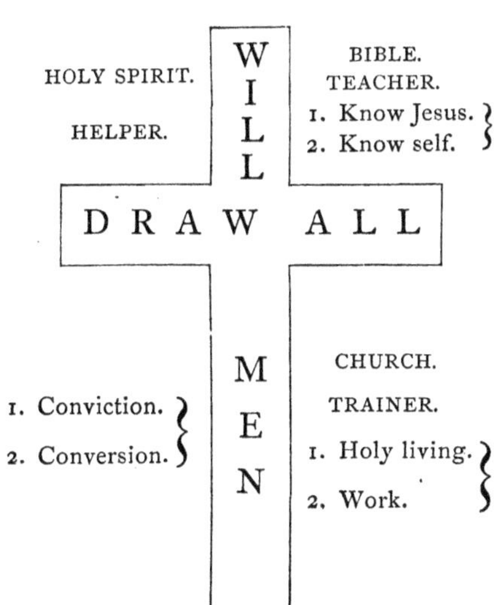

Two hearts, one bad, the other good, make an instructive lesson. Get the children to tell you what to write in them as below:

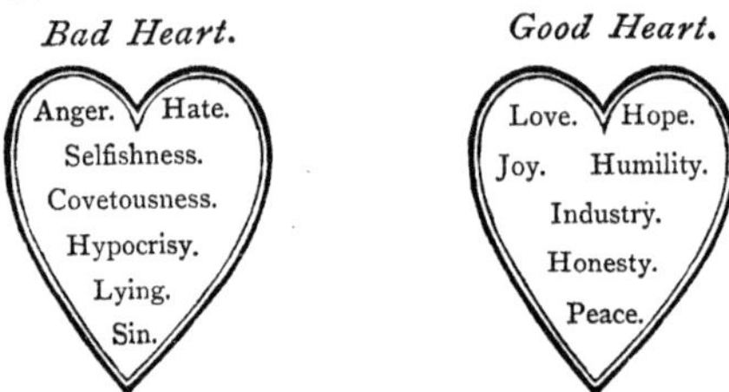

Still another is the following: "Jesus is your friend." What qualities do you want in a friend? *Answer.* He must be TRUE. Write the word T R U E on the board, and then by questioning draw out of the scholars four different and prominent characteristics of Jesus as a friend, each answering to one of the letters of the word *True*, as follows:

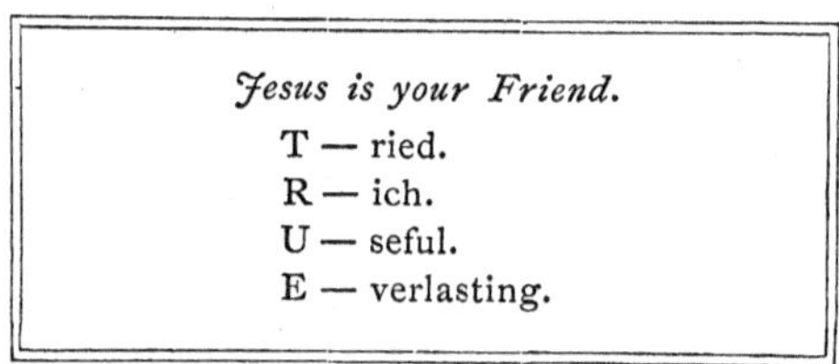

The Parable of the Sower may be taught by the following arrangement in three columns and twelve words or particulars. The *children give the words* to fill the columns:

The Soil.	What became of the Seed.	Represented what Hearers.
Wayside.	The Devil seized it.	Careless.
Stony.	The sun scorched it.	Superficial.
Thorny.	Tares choked it.	Worldly.
Good.	Fruit.	Pious.

The lesson, "Son, go work to-day in my vineyard," may be thus arranged:

Who? — "Son,
What? — go work
When? — to-day
Where? — in my vineyard."

How work? *Answer:* W — illingly.
O — rderly.
R — egularly.
K — indly.

The next three examples are from Rev. J. H. Vincent's blackboard exercises:

History of Joseph.

1.	Bo (rn 1745 B. C.	
2.	So (ld	17 years old.
3.	Imp (risoned	9 years in slavery.
4.	Rel (eased	4 years—in prison.
5.	Ber (eaved	29 years—loses his father.
6.	Di (ed	51 years.
		110 years old.

The Seven principal Journeys of Christ.

1.	Bethlehem	to Jerusalem,	6 miles north.
2.	J.	to B.	6 miles south.
3.	B.	to Eg.	250 miles S. W.
4.	E.	to Naz.	350 miles N. E.
5.	Naz.	to J	65 miles south.
6.	J.	to N.	65 miles north.
7.	N.	to Jer.	50 miles S. E.

Seven Golden Rules of Sabbath-school Order.

1st s, for silence.
2d s, for system.
1st v, for vigilance.
2d v, for variety.
1st c, for charity.
2d c, for concentration.
central C for CHRIST.

A more elaborate lesson, illustrating the parable of the Pharisee and Publican, and showing the characteristics of three kinds of prayer and their results, can be portrayed thus:

P R A Y E R.
harisee prayed proudly.
ublican prayed penitently.
oor widow prayed perseveringly.

roud prayer proved worthless.
enitent prayer procured peace.
ersevering prayer prevailed.

Another still is to write a part of the text and fill it up with the answers of the scholars, thus:

"At thy word I will {
Repent.
Pray.
Believe.
Love.
Obey.
Suffer."

A lesson on the *Beggars that cried to Jesus*, as found in Matt. xx. 30–34, may thus be placed:

What the beggars did.	cried in distress. cried with importunity. cried with faith. cried with humility.
What Jesus did.	stood still. asked what they wanted. had compassion. touched them.
Result.	He healed them. They followed him.

Map Drawing.—Palestine.

Another use for the blackboard in the Sunday-school is the drawing of maps and outlines of the location of sacred places. Teachers have found it difficult, however, if not impossible, to draw maps of the proper proportions and rightly to locate the places. The following simple plan, used by Ritter and Guyot, has been extensively used in our Sunday-school Conventions the last year or two, and found to be useful. It is called the "Relative Measurement" method. One line, say from A to B (see diagram on page 123), is taken as the unit of measurement. This line is 40 miles in length. Having drawn this line at the top or northern boundary of Palestine, next dot off five times forty miles south, and number it in proper proportions, 1, 2, 3, 4, 5. Then run three times forty miles west, and number 6, 7, and 8. Then draw a line from A, sloping to the figure 8, for the coast-line, and you have the general outline of Palestine. Then run another dotted line from A to 6, and you have the Jordan line. The River Jordan rises opposite 1. The Sea of Galilee lies opposite No. 2. The Dead Sea opposite 4 and 5. The principal mountains are designated as /\ H. for Hermon, etc. Cities by * and letters, as Jer. for Jerusalem, C. for Cæsarea, etc. (See table.)

The great divisions are made by drawing a curved line from Mount Carmel to the Jordan, midway between 2 and 3. Then equidistant between 3 and 4 draw a circular line to the coast of the Mediterranean Sea. The length of the Holy Land is about 180 miles and the width from 25 to 70 miles.

The Sea of Galilee is 12 miles long by 6 broad, and the Dead Sea is about 50 miles long. The following outline, which appeared in part in *The Sunday-School Teacher*, of Chicago, is a good illustration:

Table of Localities.

(*See Map.*)

/\ *Mountains.*	* *Cities.*	
H-ermon.	H-ebron.	N-azareth.
G-ilead.	B-ethlehem.	S-idon.
T-abor.	Jer-usalem.	T-yre.
P-isgah.	J-ericho.	
C-armel.	Jop-pa.	
E-bal.	C-æsarea.	
G-erizim.	Ca-pernaum.	

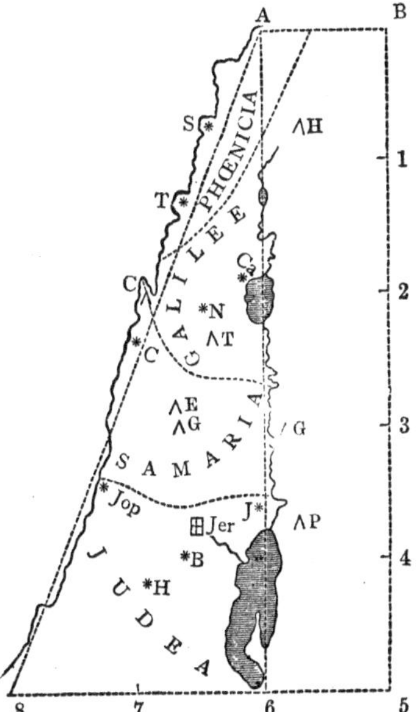

The foregoing are samples each of several classes of blackboard exercises, which I have selected as being the most practical. Other more fanciful ones are omitted, for it should ever be remembered that the true, legitimate use of the blackboard does not necessarily involve any of these ingenious devices: simply the plain Word of God, plainly written, is all.

XV.

THE INFANT-SCHOOL.

HERE is no department of the Sabbath-school work of greater importance and interest than this. We have known marked cases of hopeful conversion of children from four to seven years of age to result from the first hour of Bible instruction in the youngest infant classes. Often the character and habits of scholars as such are formed at the very first interview with their teacher, who thus meets them at the very entering in of "the gates of life." It is well known that some of our most distinguished divines, as well as active Christian ladies, date their conversion back to the early age of four, five, or six years. Therefore take measures in every Sabbath-school to organize and sustain a first-class infant-school department.

1. Get a light, warm, airy room. A lean-to added to your chapel for the purpose, or the use of the next-door neighbor's dining-room for an hour a week, will answer. Give the children a room by themselves if possible, to rise and sing, talk, recite, and pray. Furnish the room with a good black-

board and crayons, and such Scripture prints and cards and maps as you can obtain for the walls and for use. Provide for them small, comfortable seats.

2. Select and call to the charge of this class the most pious, bright, cheerful, patient, loving, gentle, winning teacher for children there is to be found in the whole church, with a like assistant. Generally the teacher will be a lady, although some men greatly excel as infant-class teachers, so that the complaining remark of the little girl to her mother, that she "hadn't any teacher to-day—it was only a *man*," was quite too severe to be just. The little ones are greatly blessed in their love for their teachers, for they want a large share of demonstrative, life-like sympathy, expressed by a soft, loving voice and a gentle manner—hands that will speak in all their gestures, and a patience that endureth and a heart that loves to teach them for Christ's sake. If the teacher feels the need of learning how to do this good work, let him visit good week-day infant-schools, and gather up suggestions and lessons, as well as confidence and inspiration, for the great work.

3. Visit and gather in all the children from the ages of three or four to seven years, whose parents are willing to send them, and at once teach them habits of punctuality, order, regularity, and pleasant worship. When they become well drilled and instructed, so that they can clearly read the Bible, then transfer them to older classes, unless there are good

reasons to the contrary. Although they are little, they are very precious, and amply worth all the pains-taking effort you can make for them.

4. Let the teacher of such a class ponder and consider the characteristics of his precious charge. 1. *Activity.*—Says Mr. Hassell, "A healthful child abhors quietude," and rightly so, as much as nature does a vacuum. Every mother knows that her little ones, if in health, "cannot bear to be still for a minute." 2. *Curiosity.*—Archbishop Whately says: "Curiosity is the parent of attention." 3. *Inquisitiveness.*—Happy is that child who is blest with a mother or teacher who will "bide patiently all the endless questionings of the little one, and will not rudely crush the rising spirit of free inquiry with an impatient nod or a frown." Rather see in their many questions but the untutored pleadings of the little ones for care and cultivation. Oh, how much they want and deserve to have their inquisitiveness satisfied by a kind, considerate answer to all their questions! 4. *Fear.*—Oh, how much children suffer from this cause! Their natural timidity should be respected, and not cruelly wrought upon. 5. Then, too, children have *wonder*, and like to talk and hear of "wonderful things." 6. They have also a proper love of approbation, and they should be cheered and encouraged when they try to do well.

Now let the teacher take up the first of these well-known characteristics, and act upon it. An excellent teacher of an infant class, some years ago, was accustomed to gain order by appealing to their *love of activity*. She would stand quietly at the desk and ask the children: "Children, will you please tell me what the gods of the heathen are like?" This was always a pleasing request to them, and every form would stand erect, with every hand by their sides, and they would together begin the part of the 115th Psalm which answers that question. They would repeat all together, "Eyes have they, but they see not," and every pair of little hands would go with the teacher's, pointing to, and resting upon, their eyes. In like manner, "mouths have they," "noses," "ears," "feet," "hands," etc., always suiting the action to the word. All are in perfect order, and the next step for the teacher would naturally be to talk a little about the gods of the heathen, and then sing a verse about "bowing down to gods of wood and stone." The transition is then natural and easy to "Our God" in heaven, where angels, saints, parents, and children too, are; and they sing the hymn to which all leads, viz.: "Around the throne of God in heaven, Thousands of children stand," etc., etc.

Another mode of conducting an infant-school is to place the children in little classes, of six scholars, with a teacher for each, and proceed with singing, repeating commandments, singing, recitation for ten minutes, study of emblems, a ten-minute address, and prayers, having a verse or two of singing between every exercise, and no exercise longer than ten minutes. Thus an excellent system of infant-class instruction proceeds, while the lady who has charge gives the address and superintends the teachers, etc., for the hour devoted to the school.

Another way is to take the two central verses of the regular lesson for the whole school and bring it out on the blackboard, and question, instruct, and pray and sing about the same thought of God in the lesson; as, "Who formed you, child, and made you live?" *Ans.* "God did my life and spirit give," etc., with singing and prayer.

Another infant-class teacher has a different plan, as follows: She has arranged with a gentleman, who teaches a large class of young ladies of sixteen to twenty years of age, to come in with his class and conduct the opening exercises of the infant-school. He then goes into another room and instructs his class for thirty minutes, and the lady instructs the children for the same time. Then the Bible-class, with their teacher, return, and the infant-school is divided into classes, in which the young ladies teach the same lesson which they have just received from their teacher. In this way practice in teaching, and variety are gained, and the lady teacher in the infant-school is relieved of a part of her burden.

I have never found two infant-class teachers who conducted their schools exactly alike. Each one has some peculiarity in his or her mode. There is no standard mode of infant-class instruction. Adaptation according to circumstances is the rule. The children should be received with great care into the infant-school, and be given to understand that it is a place for the holy worship of God, and to learn of him. The children should always be greeted by the teacher with a loving smile, that is free from every trace of giddiness, and with words of sincere, respectful welcome. Great evil is done if the teacher is cold, morose, or fretful in spirit or manner. The teacher should pray with, as well as for, the children. They may repeat the words of the prayer after the teacher; and it is well to prepare them for the act, by some such remark as, "Children, we want to thank God this morning for this holy Sabbath, for the Sabbath-school, for kind teachers, for the blessed Bible, for our God and Saviour Jesus Christ," and so on, mentioning the different objects of desire. Let the prayers always be short and simple, and sing but one, two or three verses at a time. The addresses should always be clear and suited to the children. An excellent model of scriptural talks to infant-class children will be found in "Peep of Day," "Line upon Line," and "Precept upon Precept." "The Tract Primer" and "Child's Scripture Question Book" have also some good things to work up for infant-classes. There are various other helps from which good suggestions can be gathered.

The children should recite their verse or verses simultaneously; then by benches, or classes, and then by a few individual scholars called upon, so as to ascertain if all have learned it. The time cannot be wasted by hearing each scholar recite in turn where there are only one or two teachers. Care should be taken not to burden the young mind. A small, bright, clear, pleasant Bible truth is best. As the good Dr. Ryland used to say, "Simplify and repeat: Simplify and repeat," remembering that simplicity is not poverty of expression. Learn, also, how to carry thoughts *into* a child's mind, and not leave them, as many do, at the doorway. Aim at Christ and salvation. Let no hymn be sung which you are not, beforehand, careful to see that the children really understand. Make every truth clear and simple, and let them act the lesson out with appropriate gesticulations and motions. When speaking of God, let them do it reverently, and perhaps by all pointing their little fingers upward.

Bible stories and anecdotes are generally best and most interesting for infant-classes. Use the blackboard freely with words and appropriate figures, for such little ones learn best that which they learn through the eye. Teach little at a time, but teach that little well and thoroughly, is a grand motto for the infant-class teacher.

It is of great importance that the children should always feel that their teachers are the best and happiest persons they ever saw, and that they are always so very bright and happy because the religion of Jesus makes them so full of love and joy, and they cannot help its overflow; and that they consider it the greatest privilege of life thus to tell their scholars of Jesus, and lead the little children cheerfully along Zion's road towards the heavenly Canaan.

Examples of Infant-class Lessons.

Example No. 1.

The following lesson was publicly taught by Ralph Wells before the Philadelphia Sunday-School Teachers' Institute, in September, 1867, and phonographically reported for the columns of *The Sunday-School Times.* The class was composed of some twenty children:

The Lesson.

TEACHER.—Look around just for a moment, children, and see how many people are looking at us. I want you to have one good look, and then to give me all the rest of your attention. After you have had your look, I want you to sing a little with me.. [The children face the audience for a moment, smiling, parents and teachers returning their gaze with fond affection, and shall we not say, with many prayers that the lesson might be abundantly blessed?]

Now let me see how exactly you can repeat the hymn after me. I will speak first, and you will follow me:

"Jesus loves me, this I know,"

[Children repeat, in earnest harmony.]

"For the Bible tells me so."

[Children repeat thus, after the teacher, the first stanza.]

TEACHER.—"Jesus loves me." Let us look at this a moment. We think that praying and reading the Bible, and saying the lesson are worshipping God; and so they are; but we often forget that in reading and singing these beautiful Sabbath-school hymns we are worshipping God, too.

"Jesus loves me, this I know,
For the Bible tells me so."

[After the hymn was sweetly sung, the teacher talked very pleasantly about the beautiful Letter which our dear heavenly Father has sent to us.] That Letter is the blessed Bible. We are going to have a lesson out of it to-night. But we cannot understand it unless our Father sends some one to open our hearts to understand it. We have sung a verse to him: now we will look to him in prayer and ask him to be our Teacher. [The class close their eyes, fold their hands, and repeat the prayer after their teacher.]

Dear Lord Jesus!—We thank thee for the Bible—we thank thee that it tells us—that God loves us—that he sent Jesus to die for us.—We thank thee—for all its promises;—that it tells us—if we love Jesus—and trust in him—we shall go to heaven;—that if we love Jesus—and trust in him—he will never leave us.—To-night, dear Father—send the blessed Spirit—to make us attentive—to help us to find Jesus—and what he would have us to do—and how we can get to heaven.—O dear Saviour!—sometimes when we try—we find it very hard—to do right.—Let us never be discouraged—but whenever we sin—go to Jesus and tell him all—and get his help.—Dear Jesus—help us to live for thee—to do good while we live—to be a blessing to all around us—and to show that we love thee—in our homes—to little brothers and sisters—and to all our companions—at home—at school—and everywhere.—May we so live—that everybody shall see—that we are Jesus' little lambs.—Hear our prayer—and come to-night and be our Teacher—and may our little hearts—to-night—be given away to Jesus—to love and serve him—as long as we live.—We ask for Jesus' sake.—Amen.

[This simple petition was offered by the children, as with one voice, the tone and accentuation of the leader being caught up and carried by them with affecting earnestness of pleading. One could not but feel that the exercise was *real*, with both teacher and class.]

TEACHER.—Now sing with me one verse more, children, and we will take a Bible lesson together. It is new to you, but we sung it over once this afternoon, and I guess you can sing it now. I will sing one verse for you, because it is new to you, and then we will sing it together. It begins with

"Oh, I must be a lover of the Lord!"

Let me sing it for you. [Teacher sings.]

"Oh, I must be a lover of the Lord,
Oh, I must be a lover of the Lord,
Oh, I must be a lover of the Lord,
Or I can't go to heaven when I die."

[The children then sing it with Mr. Wells, and finally by themselves, clearly, loudly and accurately.]

There is a little sentence of only four words, children, that has been more precious to me than any other in the world. I wrote it on a piece of paper years ago, and put it in my pocket-book—here it is, with little flowers around it—[Producing it and holding it up to the class.] Would you like me to give you these four words? *Yes, sir!* Well, I will write them on the board. [Writes:]

Christ died for me.

I do not know whether you can read—[the children, quickly interrupting, read "*Christ died for me.*"] Yes, if ever this world loves Jesus, it will be because these four little words get into everybody's heart. Try and remember them.

I am now going to read a verse out of our Father's Letter. It is a sad story. After I read it, I am going to tell it to you in my way; and after I have told it to you, I am going to ask you, to see if you can tell me all about it. Then I am going to tell you the meaning; then the lesson—three things: the story, the meaning, the lesson. Can you give them to me? First, the—*story*, next, the—*meaning*, and last, the—*lesson*, [the children say.] Once more, give them to me.—*Story*, *meaning*, *lesson*.

I will read it first out of the Bible, for I always want to give you God's word first; then I will tell it to you. It is in the twelfth chapter of the Book of Exodus. "Exodus" means the "going out." When you leave this room you "go out" of it—it is your "Exodus" of the room. So, in the Bible story, God's people went out. Let me read to you:

"Then Moses called for all the elders of Israel, and said unto them, Draw out and take you a lamb according to your families, and kill the passover. And ye shall take a bunch of hyssop, and dip it in the blood that is in the basin, and strike the lintel and the two side-posts with the blood that is in the basin; and none of you shall go out at the door of his house until the morning. For the Lord will pass through to smite the Egyptians; and when he seeth the blood upon the lintel, and on the two side-posts, the Lord will pass over the door, and will not suffer the destroyer to come in unto your houses to smite you."

And it happened just as God said. Now, I do not want to tell you anything that you can tell me. In the first place, we want to find out where this took place. Can any of you tell me the name of the country? [*Egypt!* shout three or four little voices—to the surprise even of the teacher, who, as well as the audience, was repeatedly astonished at the accuracy, promptness, and clearness of the children's answers.]

The Israelites, or God's people, are spoken of in the lesson. They are now in Egypt. Let me mark it on the board. Here is *Egypt*, [drawing a rough outline of the Red Sea, river Nile, and the Mediterranean; and, proceeding northerly, of Palestine.] Pointing to the latter, the teacher said, Here is—*Canaan*, one child replied. Yes! that little girl has it. And what city is this? [making a dot near the corner of the Dead Sea.] Je-*rusalem!* [a little boy finishes the word.] God's people had been dwelling in Canaan; how did they come to be in Egypt, where we find them in our lesson? Who first went down to get corn? *Joseph.* Yes. There was no corn in the land. What do you call it when there is nothing to eat? *Famine!* a bright boy replies. Very well, indeed. Who, then, went first to buy corn? *Joseph.* And who followed him? *His brethren.* What did they go for?—to keep them from—*Starving!* That is it, exactly. I like to hear children answer so well. Can any of you tell me how many Israelites or Jews there were in Egypt? How many is that? [Writing the figures 2,000,000 on the board.] *Two million!* [eagerly responded a little fellow, who certainly did credit to his week-day instructors.] Yes, there were probably two million—men, women, and children. What was the name of the king of Egypt? It begins with P.—*Pharaoh.* Yes, God said to him, "Let my people—*go.*" but Pharaoh said, "I—*won't!*" Then God said, "I will show him what I will do. My people shall go, that they may serve me." So God told his people to get ready that night, when our lesson begins.

What should you think this was? [Drawing a rough figure of the face of a clock.] *A clock.* Yes. What hour is the hand pointing to? *Twelve o'clock.* What time of night do you call that? *Midnight.* Yes, at midnight God said he would go from house to house in the land of Egypt, and every house where he did not see something on the door he would go in and kill the first-born. Let us make a door, now. [Drawing the outline of a door.] We won't take time to draw it very nicely. "Every house where I see something on the door," God said. What was it he must see on the door? *Blood! blood!* [Taking the red crayon, spots of red are dotted here and there over the white door-posts, representing blood.] Yes; wherever I see the blood of a little killed lamb on the door, I will not go in and slay the first-born.

This blood must first be in a—[Drawing an outline of a bowl or basin,]—*Basin,* the children reply. Yes; and how are you to get the blood on the door? [Taking the green chalk, and drawing a bush.] Here is a little bush, called hyssop, something like a huckleberry bush, and the people were to take that and dip it in the basin, into the blood, and do what? *Sprinkle it on the door!* Yes. What part of the door? (A pause.) L-i-n-t-e-l; what does that spell? *Lintel.*

Then, "when I see the—*blood*—on the—*lintel*—and on the two—*side-posts*—I will not go in and—*kill the first-born!*" Yes. That was what God said.

I have sometimes thought I could see an Egyptian soldier that night with his armor on, going up to one of the Israelites and asking, "What is that you are putting on the door?" "It is some lamb's blood." "What are you putting it on for?" "Because my God has told me to." Then with a strut he has turned on his heel and walked away, muttering to himself, "What a big fool that Jew is!"

But see! the hands on the clock begin to get around. It is now pointing to—*midnight.* Yes, pretty soon it strikes one—two—three, up to—*twelve.* And then! Oh! the angel of death went from one house to another, and in every one that didn't have—*the blood*—on it, the first-born was—*killed.* Yes! And one wail of woe went up from Egypt that night. Fathers and mothers, from Pharaoh in his beautiful palace, to his poorest servant, were weeping and wailing and lamenting their first-born, slain by the hand of the angel of God.

But some houses escaped. The ones with the—*blood* on.

Had there been any death in those houses? *No, sir.* Think. What had died? *A little lamb.* Yes; a little lamb had been killed and his blood put in—*a basin.* And then—suppose the basin had been set behind the door, would that have done? *No, sir.* The blood must be sprinkled on the —*door,* and it must be sprinkled by a bunch of—*hyssop.* Yes; it must all be done exactly as God had said. Then the door that had the blood upon it was passed over by the angel, was it? *Yes, sir.* And what was done to the house where there was no blood? What did the angel do? *Went in.* Yes, and—*slew the first-born.* [Mr. Wells then called a little boy up to the board, drew a rough sketch of three or four door-frames, on two of which he used the red chalk, making marks to represent blood. The boy was then asked, with the class, to point out which houses the angel would enter, and which pass over, thus drilling the fact impressively and perfectly into the scholars' minds, as also the reason for the angel's choice—the *blood* of the lamb.]

How do you think I got here? *On the cars.* What drew the cars? *An engine.* Did you ever see an engine? *Yes, sir!* (with emphasis). This summer, where I live, at Tarrytown, a gentleman said to me, "Don't you want to go down on the track and see the express train go by to-night?" I said yes: so we went. By-and-by I heard a rumble: it seemed to come nearer and nearer, and got louder and louder. What was coming? *The express train.* Yes, it was going to rush by us at thirty miles an hour. Could we have held out our hands and stopped it? *No, sir!* (emphatically, and incredulously). Suppose we had had you to help us, could we then? *No, sir!* Well, suppose all the people in this house had caught hold of the cars?—what then? *It would have pulled them to pieces!* [a little girl says]. Well, in a minute or two I heard a sharp *toot! toot!*—what was that? *The whistle.* Yes, and the man on the engine put his hand on a little iron bar and pushed it, and the cars began to go slower and slower and slower until they stopped. The man put his hand on the right place, the place of power, the place that made the engine go or stop. Now, what does Jesus say to us? "Behold, I stand at the door and knock." Can you tell me at what door Jesus knocks? *Our hearts.* "If any man," or child, "will hear my voice, and open—*the door*—I will come in and—*sup with him.*" Yes, "and he with me;" and we shall be saved. But there must be something on the door, or we cannot be saved, any more than the Jews, if they forgot, or would not, put the blood on the doors of their houses. What must *we* have on the door? *Blood.* Yes. Well, will it do if you cut your finger, and sprinkle the blood on your house? *No, sir.* Suppose you kill a little lamb, and put the blood on your front door, will that save you? *No, sir, no, sir!* What must the blood be on? *Our hearts!* Yes, the blood must be put upon the right place, the place where Jesus knocks, the place of power. Our hearts then are—*the door.* And what must be sprinkled on the door? *Blood.*

Why did our soldiers go off to the war? *To fight;* yes, and to shed their—*blood*—for their country. And what does shedding their blood mean? *They died*—[a little girl answers]. Right; they shed their blood, they died for our country. Jesus shed his blood, That means the same as Jesus—*died;* yes; how? *On the cross.* He hung there for you, did he? *Yes, sir.* And for me? *Yes, sir;* and for us all? A little girl in a mission-school, named Mary, sat on the front seat, and when the superintendent was telling about how they hanged Jesus on the cross, the tears came to her eyes, and when he got to where they took the hammer and the nails to nail him, little Mary could not stand it any longer, but she had to get up and go out. In the afternoon she came back smiling, and the superintendent asked her, "Mary, where did you go this morning?" and she said, "Oh, teacher, I could not stand it when you spoke to us about Jesus being nailed on the cross, for I felt just as if I helped to pound the nails in, and I went off a little piece from the school, and got down on my knees and told Jesus that my sins helped to hang him on the cross, and I asked him to please forgive me for helping to kill him—that I was so sorry; but now I feel so happy." Jesus forgave her, and to-day Mary is a little Christian girl.

I have something in my pocket (drawing out a roll) that I want you to see. Years ago I went thousands of miles away, and I sent on to Washington and got this paper, It is called a "passport." There is the great seal of the United States on it, and here is the Secretary's signature at the bottom. And when I was away, in strange countries, where I could not speak the language, all I had to do was to show this paper, and they said, "Let him pass," or something that meant that, and I was allowed to go on. If I had not had this passport, I could not have got through. The blood of Jesus must be our passport. When God sees this blood sprinkled on the door of our hearts, he will say, "Let him pass," and we will be allowed to go through this life in safety, and get to heaven when we die. But oh, how many times we have to use this passport! How often we sin and need to come to Jesus for forgiveness, and to point to his precious blood sprinkled on our hearts!

The teacher further continued the lesson, illustrating by pointed and affecting incidents, briefly recapitulating, and closing with a short prayer, in which the little ones feelingly joined. The above is all that need be quoted to give an idea of the style of this successful teacher of the children..

Example No. 2.

The following lesson was kindly forwarded to the author, in manuscript, from London, by the young lady teacher, "S. E. A.," who has been remarkably successful in public exercises of teaching very young children.

A Lesson upon Forgiveness.

Harry and Fred went to school. They had to cross a road to get to it. A boy used to stand at the crossing with a broom in his hand to sweep it with; this boy was very rude to Harry and Fred: he used to try and keep them from crossing the road. Once he took away Fred's books and splashed him with mud. When the boy saw Harry and Fred running and making haste, lest they should be late at school, he would be sure to stop them. In the winter-time he made them walk upon the snow. Sometimes he held up his broom before their faces and cried out, "Can't come across, can't come across; you'll be late, you'll have the stick." Then, again, when they were very early, he would tell them they were late, and so make them run. At last, one day all the children of the school to which Harry and Fred went were going to take flowers to their teacher, as it was her birthday. Henry said that he would bring a beautiful nosegay, for his papa's gardener was going to cut him a large one from the green-house for him to take to school. Well, the morning of the birthday came: the school-children brought a great many beautiful flowers; Harry and Fred did not come with the rest; the children wondered where they could be. At last though, in they came, but no nosegay: they made a bow, said "Good-morning," and then both looked down on the ground. "Where's your nosegay?" said a little girl to Harry. "I have not got one," he answered. How could that have happened? The gardener had cut them a beautiful large nosegay, and when they left home in the morning for school they had it with them—what had become of it? Had the boy taken it away? I will tell you all about it. As they were running along very fast to get to school in time, all at once they left off running and began to walk slowly. They were near the crossing, and they felt afraid of the boy; they need not have been frightened, for the boy was sitting down on a doorstep crying, with his head resting upon his knees, and took no notice of them. As they were going past him, Harry said, "Oh, he will not hurt us; let us stop; I wonder what he is crying for?" "What is the matter?" said Fred to him. "Mind your own business," answered the boy; "go on to school." So on they went, but as they turned away the boy saw the nosegay, and called after them to come back. "Don't go." said Fred: "he's a wicked boy; we can't help him." Well, they were going on when Harry looked again and saw him crying; so he and Fred turned back: then the boy told them that he was very hungry, that his mother and grandmother were both at home very hungry and ill, that a policeman had turned him away from his crossing, and he had not earned any money for three days. Harry said, "Poor fellow!" and he wished he had a penny to give the poor boy. Then Harry and Fred looked at their flowers; the boy looked too. "He can't have our flowers, you know," said Fred; "we want them for our teacher, she is so kind, and I want to show how much I love her." So they walked off slowly, and the boy looked after them and the nosegay as if he would like very much to have it. "I say he does not deserve to be helped," said Fred. "So do I," said Harry; "and then these flowers are too good to give to him." However, they did not feel quite comfortable, and then they remembered a text they had learned at school the day before—"*If ye forgive not men their trespasses, neither will your Father forgive your trespasses.*" That is, dear children, if we do not forgive others, God will not forgive us. So Harry said, "Here, Fred! take the flowers to him." Fred took the flowers, went up to the boy, put them in his hand, and then ran away. A gentleman soon after gave the boy a shilling for the nosegay, and I dare say you can guess what he did with it. When Harry and Fred gave the nosegay to the boy, it made them feel very happy—more happy than if they had given it to their teacher; and it did the boy good too: their kindness made all his rudeness go away, and always after this day he did all he could to please Harry and Fred.

Tell me the names of the boys I have spoken to you about? *How* did the crossing-sweeper behave to them? *What* were they going to take to school one day? *Why? Did* Harry and Fred take their nosegay to school? *What* did they do with it? *Did* the boy deserve to have it? *Why* did they give it to him then? Yes, they gave it to him to show that they had forgiven him. Sometimes people are unkind to you; perhaps one day a boy went up to you James, and stole your marbles; perhaps your big sister one day gave you a slap, Mary. Now, if she ever slaps you again, or if the boy takes away James's marbles again, are you to hit them and call them hard names, or to forgive them? *Why?* Yes, you should forgive them because God wishes you to do so; because it will be acting like Jesus to do so; because God will not forgive you if you do not forgive. Let us think a little about Jesus. You know that one evening when he was praying in a quiet garden, some wicked men came and dragged him away; you remember how the soldiers mocked him, took off his clothes, put on him an old robe, a make-believe crown made of thorns—dared to be so filthy as to spit in his face, beat him; and then they put great nails through his hands and through his feet, and nailed him to a cross of wood, put it up and let him hang there. How the nails must have torn his hands!—what great pain they must have given him! You know if a pin were put through your flesh how the pain would make you cry out; what then must have been the pain of the nails! And then he did not deserve this cruel treatment: he had gone about doing good. If any persons deserved to be punished, those who put Jesus, the kind, loving Saviour, to death, deserved to be; and Jesus could have punished them if he had chosen, for he was God's dear Son; but no, he did not punish them. Instead of that, he prayed for them: he said, "Father, forgive them; for they know not what they do!" Let us ask God, the Holy Spirit, to give us a forgiving spirit, and so make us like Jesus.

Here is a story which Jesus once told, that he might teach us to forgive others: A king once had a servant who owed him ten thousand pieces of money. When the king called the servant that he might pay back the money, the servant had nothing to pay: not even one piece of money could he pay back, and he owed—ten thousand. Then the king ordered that the servant and his wife and children should be sold as slaves, and work until there was enough money to pay back the ten thousand pieces. When the servant heard this he fell down on his face before the king, and said, "Lord, have patience with me, and I will pay thee all;" in other words, "Do wait a little longer and I will pay back all the money." Suppose Alfred's mother owes the baker for a great many loaves, and he was to come to her house one day and say, "I must have my money; I won't go away till you pay it to me;" and then your mother were to cry, and tell him how sorry she was she had no money, but that the children had been ill, and that she had had to give all her money to the doctor, but that if he would wait a week longer she would get the money and pay him. Well, suppose the baker was to feel quite sorry for your mother, and should say, "Well, I won't ask you for the money: you need not pay me at all. I will give you the bread you've had." Now, that is what this king did. The servant said, "Wait a little longer and I will pay you." The king said, "You need not pay me at all: I forgive you it all." The servant went away. As he was going away he met a man who owed him a hundred pennies: he went up to him, laid hold of him very rudely by the throat, and said, "Pay me what you owe me!"

The man fell down at his feet, and said, "Have patience with me, and I will pay you all." *How* much money had the king just forgiven the servant? *How* much did this man owe the servant? *What* ought he to have done? But he did not forgive him, but had him put in prison directly. Some servants were standing by and saw what this unkind servant had done, so they went to the king and told him all about it. He ordered the servant to be brought back before him, and then the king said to him, "O you wicked servant I forgave you all that debt: ought you not to have forgiven the poor man what he owed you?" The king was very angry with him, and had him put in prison until he paid the very last farthing. Then Jesus told the people to whom he was speaking that so their heavenly Father would not forgive them if they would not forgive one another.

How many pieces of money did the servant owe his lord? *Had* he any money to pay back with? *What* did the king order to be done to him and his wife and children? *What* did the servant then say? *Did* the king give him a little longer time? *How* much did a man owe this servant? *Tell* me how he treated the man? *Who* went and told the king all about it? *What* did the king *say* to the servant? *What* did he *do* to him? *Who* was it prayed for those who treated him so cruelly? *Now*, when you go home, I want you to tell your mothers and fathers about the lesson. Repeat it. If we do not forgive others, God will not forgive us. Try and remember three things—about Harry and Fred; the king and the servant; the Lord Jesus.

XVI.

YOUNG MEN AND WOMEN'S BIBLE-CLASSES.

WE can hardly find words to convey our impression of the surpassing importance of these classes. To train teachers, to train mothers and fathers, to restrain from doubtful company, and to furnish good companions and Christian associations, reading, habits, impulses to the young men and women of this generation, is a work worthy of the highest aspirations of the best and noblest of our race. If we look at the census, we cannot fail to notice the striking fact that a little more than *one-third* of the entire population of New York are young men and women over fifteen and under thirty years of age, while more than one-half of our population is under twenty years of age.

In a very short time the destinies of our country and of our churches will be in the hands of these young people. To a large extent they have been neglected in the family, in society, in the Sabbath-school, and in the Church; and as Dr. James W. Alexander said: "Be it ever remembered, that the neglecters of the Church have been neglected by the Church." These young people can no longer be petted as children, and they are not generally treated with the respect due to them as rising young men and women. Said a youth of fifteen once: "Uncle, I don't know what I can do with myself. I am too old to play with children, and I am not old enough to be interesting to the older people." This anomalous position such young people sadly feel. They are sensitive, beyond any other period of life, to any slight or neglect, and after a vain struggle to gain a recognition and position anywhere, they rush to the gilded saloons or the giddy dance for that sympathy, kindness, and regard which they vainly seek for in the family, the Sabbath-school and the Church of Christ.

This should never be, and it must not be. But can these persons be reached and gained by the Sabbath-school? And how? After due consideration, I reply, in the first place, that they *can* be reached. My reasons are:

1. Because earnest, warm-hearted, disinterested efforts in this direction have ever been successful. When building the Brick Church in Rochester, N. Y., the names of all the scholars and their ages were transcribed and placed in the corner-stone, when it was ascertained that, of the whole number—I think 652—the average age was fourteen years and ten months; and other churches in that city present a similar record, because the able and influential

Christian business men and women of Rochester devote themselves to this great work.

2. Because no class of persons is more susceptible to kind attention and real sympathy. They are quick to perceive and prompt to act. No class is more hopeful.

3. Because these senior classes, when appropri ately conducted, are well adapted to meet the wants of their personal, social, intellectual, and religious nature, and to fill a secret void that is keenly felt by these precious youth.

In the second place, *How* can our young men and women be reached? I answer:

1. Christian men and women of real talent and character, of religious and social position, must be thoroughly aroused to a self-sacrificing, devoted, heartfelt interest for them. They must put their hearts into it. No feigned respect will do. Nothing but real sympathy will be received. No mere professions will answer. These youth are quick and sharp-sighted to detect anything insincere or unreal. The best men and women of our churches must be chosen to take charge of their classes—persons who can and will understand, appreciate, and respect young people. They must evince a more anxious and watchful desire to notice and approve what is right in them, than to condemn that which is wrong. They must be patient and forbearing, with a good control of their countenance, tone of voice, language, quick to discover the value and bearing of the half-

uttered opinions of the class, with an earnest personal interest in each one and all things that concern them. They should be enabled to prove themselves sincere friends and counsellors of all—both for this life, in employment, business, social questions, amusements, etc., and for the life that is to come. They should have an intelligent enthusiasm in the great work, with a strong faith in God, in his Word, and in his Spirit, and a hearty good-will to man.

2. Lay your plans for these classes on so large and liberal a scale as to command the scholars' respect as well as your own. Render them as pleasant and as attractive as possible. Make the best arrangements you can as to room, seats, library, and periodicals. I am sure *The Sunday-School Times* and other Sabbath-school journals and magazines, would be very useful in such a service. Do all you can to raise these classes in their own estimation, and omit no opportunity to cherish self-respect on the part of each member, and try to inspire them all with higher aspirations and better hopes. Manifest, as well as feel, a *personal* interest in each one.

3. Aim high and direct. Have a distinct, definite aim and object in all your teachings, and see that each member of the class clearly understands it. Young people want drawing out and leading forward in gentle confidence. In these classes we ought to select and train for the purpose our best Sabbath-school teachers. If the exercises are allowed to degenerate into unprofitable discussions, the ex-

mination of curious questions, controversies, or skeptical subjects, they may be productive of positive evil. Care should be taken, therefore, to engross them with the most ennobling themes. None can better appreciate what is truly excellent than these young people. An appeal to the Word and to the Testimony they will understand and respect. Lead them to compare Scripture with Scripture. Illustrate the Old Testament from the New, and also bring illustration for the New Testament from the Old. Induce the young people to make the best use of a good reference Bible, searching out parallel passages for comparison, inference, and illustration, and all will be interested and benefited. Use similes, metaphors, etc., which so abound, as well as comparisons and inferences. The following quotation may serve as an illustration of four figures of speech, all brought into one sentence:

"Imagine a father bewailing the loss of his son, by drowning.

Simile—He stood firmly upon the beach, like an oak of the forest,

Metaphor—and cried out, with trumpet voice,

Hyperbole—louder than the cannon's roar:—

Apostrophe—Oh ocean! thou hast robbed me of a beloved and courageous son."

4. The character, interests, and feelings of the class should be the teacher's unwearied, daily study. This will be a noble work. Nothing which concerns them should be treated by the teacher with indiffer-

ence. His profoundest thoughts, reading, observation, and study should be laid under contribution to his class. Painstaking saves thousands, neglect ruins millions. Count no sacrifice too dear to win souls.

5. It is indispensable that the teacher of such a class should always be courteous. Religion should at least make its possessor a gentleman, and this the young people all know right well. His whole life and bearing will influence the little circle. The personal appearance also should be duly regarded. Says a teacher: "The manner of a teacher should always be marked by these qualities: 1. Animation—a quickened, active state of the whole soul; 2. Intention—the aim and endeavor to impart the information required; 3. Earnestness—zeal in executing the instruction."

6. The class should be consulted, as far as possible, respecting the subject of study. The teacher should lose no opportunity to evince his respect for their opinions. His difficult questions should be asked generally of the class, while the personal questions should be easy and adapted. He should receive all their answers with an abounding charity and confidence, and make the most of the feeblest responses. A tart reply to a single remark will ofttimes seal the lips and hearts of a whole class. They love confidence, and become afraid to trust a teacher with their stammering, half-uttered, imperfect answers, particularly if he appears more anxious

to be smart and witty than to do them good and honor them. Let the lessons be systematic and complete. The teacher should aim to draw out the thoughts of his pupils in an easy way, instead of pouring in his own. "*Thoughts*, not words," should be the class-motto, and none can appreciate them better than young people. Let the illustrations be well-chosen and appropriate. If you strike an important practical question during the lesson, do not leave it until satisfactorily investigated, whether the lesson is covered or not. Let every mind be calm and unembarrassed, so that it will work well; much depends upon the class, as well as upon the capacity of the teacher. "A few pebbles, a piece of leather, and a cord, are in some hands, a more formidable weapon than the sword of a giant, although it be strong as a weaver's beam and keen as a blade of Damascus steel."

7. These young people should be especially induced to look into their own hearts, and study their own mental and moral mechanism. Lead them often to converse about themselves. It has been truly said, that "it is a law of human nature, that man is interested in nothing so much as about himself."* Whatever relates to his own personal experience always claims his especial regard. Many quite fail as teachers, as well as preachers, because they are so impersonal.

8. Social meetings of the class should be held now and then, and pains should be taken to make them

attractive and useful. Young men and women must have their social nature regarded. The teacher should on such occasions strive to recall the freshness and vivacity of his own youth, and live it over again; enter into it heartily, and show the class his acquaintance and sympathy with all their peculiar wants, fears, and trials. Band the young people together, in social bonds and mutual pledges if you please, to attend church, prayer-meeting, and Sabbath-school, to read the Bible and pray *regularly*, and perhaps pledge also against improper reading, associates, games, drinking, smoking, late hours, neglect of the Sabbath, and unite them in associated literary efforts, in tract missions, Sabbath-school work, in visitation, and in all ways of doing good. There should be social prayer-meetings of the class at convenient times. Have, also, a well-chosen library for them, and point out from time to time the books best adapted to peculiar wants and circumstances.

9. Give each pupil distinctly to understand that every step in your efforts on his behalf is intended to lead him to Christ; that all there is to be desired in this life and in that which is to come, is embodied in this idea; that you expect, as soon as they get their minds clear upon the glad tidings of the gospel, that they will embrace them at once. Life is short, and there is no time to lose. Besides, young people when convinced are generally prompt to act, and therefore there is great encouragement. In fact,

no field of benevolent effort is more full of hope and encouragement than this one of which we speak. In a Bible-class in one of our church Sabbath-schools not long since, fifty-five persons united with that church during the current year; and in another church and class, *fifty*, and in another still, *thirty-four*—all as the results of one year's labor. How glorious! Let then our sons and daughters, our clerks, scholars, and servant-girls, all be gathered without delay by the churches of Christ into these adult classes. Thus let the warm, burning influences of the living teacher reach every youthful heart. Says an earnest worker: "Among persons of all ages, truth most frequently has power when spoken by the living voice. The words of a teacher's mouth should be ever warm with the Spirit's breath, and strong with the vital impulses of his throbbing heart. Such words children feel." In the language of one of our Bible commentators, the truth evidently is this: "*That personal effort for the souls of individuals* —the lip, the thought, and the heart of a living man —brought into contact with the lip, thought, and heart of a living man, IS A GRAND INSTITUTION OF GOD FOR THE CONVERSION OF THE WORLD."

There is such a great necessity for adapting each lesson perfectly to the age, acquirements, etc., of the scholar, that I add a single specimen lesson from "The Sunday Teachers' Treasury." It is upon the same subject as that taken up in Mr. Wells's infant-class lesson—"The Passover"—and is given that, by comparison of style, the adaptation of the same lesson to infant and Bible-classes may be seen:

Specimen Lesson for a Senior Class.

The Feast of the Passover.

(Exodus xii.)

Circumstances of the Israelites at this time; how solemn, how stirring, how intense in interest! The institution of the Passover seems to have a threefold design. It was—1. An act of faith and obedience on the part of Israel. 2. A memorial of their deliverance. 3. A type of Christ. In the last view we will study it to-day, looking less closely at those points which we had on a former occasion, and connecting with the actual celebration of the Passover that which God connected with it—the feast of unleavened bread and the offering of the first-fruits of the barley harvest.

The Passover, then, was a type of Christ.

I. The victim was to be a lamb; and this title is applied to Christ (John i. 29).

The first altar exhibits a lamb slain; the first act of God for Israel is the slaying of the lamb; the first deed of the new dispensation was presenting, and then offering, the Lamb; the first opening of the sanctuary above, shows the "Lamb that was slain."

1. Without blemish (Matt. xxvii. 4; 1 Pet. i. 19; Heb. vii. 26).

2. Set apart four days (ver. 3, 6; John xii. 1, 12).

3. Roasted with fire (Isa. liii.; Ps. xxii.; Luke xxii. 44).

4. Not a bone to be broken (John xix. 33).

5. All the congregation were to take part (ver. 6; Matt. xxvi. 1; Acts ii. 23-36).

6. The blood was to be shed and sprinkled. Where? On the side-post and upper door-post; not on the floor, where it would be trampled on (compare 1 Pet. i. 19; Heb. x. 29).

It is not enough that Christ's blood is shed; it must be sprinkled on our hearts (Heb. xii. 24; 1 Pet. i. 2). The act of sprinkling it upon the door-posts was equivalent to a profession, "I am the Lord's." It was the means of safety, "When *I see the blood*," etc.

What encouragement for timid Christians! Perhaps, as the angel went on his awful mission, the shriek and wail from some neighboring house would reach the ears of an Israelitish family. A mother might tremble and clasp her child to her breast with fear; her faith might be weak; but if the blood were on the door she was safe, though trembling. "When I see the blood, I will pass over you." "Pass over." The general idea that God was passing through by his destroying angel, and left those doors on which the blood was seen. This, perhaps, is not strictly the meaning. At least, Bishop Lowth, an eminent Hebrew scholar, says: "Two agents are supposed—the destroying angel on his errand of judgment, and Jehovah Himself, as it were, accompanying him; and when he sees the sign, 'springing forward before the door,' he makes Himself the safety of his own" (compare Isa. xxxi. 5).

Peculiar beauty of the type thus viewed. If the blood of the Lamb is sprinkled upon us, we are as safe, though not yet as happy, as the redeemed in heaven (Rom. viii. 1, 31, 33, 34). Nothing but the blood of the great Sacrifice will save the soul. Have you come to it? No outward membership, no self-denial, no suffering, nothing but Christ can save.

II. The paschal sacrifice was to be eaten. 1. The blood was to be sprinkled *before* the food was eaten. It was consciousness of safety through the blood that enabled them with gladness to partake of the feast. We must have faith in Jesus before we can have communion with him.

2. It was to be eaten with bitter herbs and unleavened bread—the former the emblem of their bitter oppression and

the type of sorrow for sin; the latter showing that the redeemed must be holy. They are set free, but it is to be made pure.

III. The Passover was to be kept.

The feast of unleavened bread was to last seven days. It was, as it were, the continuance of the Passover. The one exhibits the *way* of pardon; the other, the holiness which follows pardon.

IV. In closing our subject, not exhausting it, turn to Leviticus xxiii. 9–11.

1. "On the morrow after the Sabbath," that is, the first day after Passover Sabbath, sometimes the third day after the Passover, sometimes later.

2. The sheaf is evidently "Christ the first-fruits" (1 Cor. xv. 23). Jesus rose the third day after the Passover, and this has become our Sabbath ever since.

3. The first sheaf is the pledge of our resurrection—that is, of our declared acceptance and full freedom by our resurrection (1 Cor. xv. 20).

How full the meaning of the apostle's words, "Christ *our Passover* is sacrificed for us, therefore let us keep the feast!" Ours is a greater danger, a nobler deliverance, a higher ransom, a grander freedom. Let us live as those who are not their own, but are redeemed from "vain conversation" as well as from death and condemnation.

XVII.

THE ART OF SECURING ATTENTION.

VERY one will acknowledge the indispensable necessity of a teacher's securing good attention. By attention we mean "fixity of thought, steadiness of mind."

1. Says Mr. Fitch: "Attention is—1. An act of the *will.* 2. It is *the one* of all the mental faculties which is most under our control. Therefore the degree of attention we give depends upon our disposition, and is therefore largely a matter of *discipline*, and other things being equal, that teacher will gain the best attention who has most personal influence, and who is looked up to with the greatest respect." (Teacher! is your character, conduct, and manner such as will entitle you to respect?) "3. Attention is a *habit.* If truly given, every day it becomes the easier. And every day we listen languidly to a lesson or sermon the habit of inattention is strengthened."

2. Attention is promoted by a deep and earnest interest in and sympathy with the child, as well as for him. We must enter into sympathy with him,

so as to understand his nature, his weaknesses, and his trials, and make all due allowance for them.

3. If the teacher would secure attention, he must be *accurately and abundantly prepared;* for no teacher can teach all he knows, and the moment a teacher approaches the limit of his preparation, he shows his weakness and embarrassment, the child detects it, and he is gone.

4. Improve well the circumstances which surround the daily life of the child, for you must here gather your best illustrations. Teachers can do this, if they are industrious, and will keep their "Sunday-school spectacles on."

5. Give the children frequent change of posture to relieve them. Study to do this especially in infant-classes. Give much freedom of motion and gesture to the little ones. If they speak of God and heaven, let them point and look upward in harmony, and thus teach them in a reverent manner to *act out* their words and feelings.

6. Simultaneous reading and making of ellipses, leaving the children to fill in a word at the close of the sentence or lesson, will aid in securing attention.

7. Recapitulation is very important to gain the attention. The scholar must give attention to be prepared for the expected review. Therefore always ask in detail, in order to see that all is understood. No child or man ever takes pains to grasp a subject, so as to fasten it in his memory, unless he expects to be called upon for it, or in some way to find use for

it hereafter. We cannot retain in our minds isolated or abstract knowledge. Todd beautifully says, "Ask a child if he knows what whiteness is, and he will tell you no; ask him if he knows what a white wall or white paper is, and he knows at once. Ask him if he knows what hardness is, and he will only stare at you; but ask him if he knows what a hard wall, or hard hand, or a hard apple is, and he will tell you at once." Connect the lesson with previous knowledge, and take great care to sustain attention with abundant resources, for if it is once lost, it is a very difficult thing to regain it on the same lesson.

8. *Pictorial* power. Word-painting by the aid of the imagination and ample details; the power of describing scenes and incidents, so as to appear real to the child's imagination, will assist you in gaining his attention. If you will dwell on all the little details of a fact clearly, you will be graphic in picturing it out in words; and without these details, the teacher may sometimes be very graphic with children, even in the simple act of reading with suitable *emotion*, *emphasis*, and *action*. Said a little girl, "Oh, father, Mr. F., the minister, read the 21st chapter of Revelation in church to-day, and it was just as if he had taken a pencil and paper and pictured it right out before us." It is St. John's elegant description of the Holy City. The Bible makes great use of the imagination in its numerous emblems, metaphors, similes, etc. In fact, we cannot worship God without the aid of the imagination. God is

compared to a sun and shield; a rock and refuge. Heaven itself is described with its streets and harps and crowns of gold, its arches, mansions, rivers, etc. Even our divine Redeemer calls himself the vine, the tree, the lamb, the bread, and fountain of living waters.

9. Avoid a stereotyped or routine mode of teaching. If ever so good, strive to improve it; vary it, and freshen it up in some way, and thus keep each child expecting something.

10. Awaken *curiosity*. Archbishop Whately says: "Curiosity is the parent of attention; and a teacher has no more right to expect success from those who have no curiosity to learn, than a husbandman has who sows a field without ploughing it;" duly regard their love of *approbation* by cherishing their self-respect; and if you would retain attention, patiently cultivate their *inquisitiveness*, for it will prove one of the grateful rewards for your kindness. Says an old writer: "The general occupation of infancy is to *inquire*. Education *directs* their *inquiries*." Therefore, bear patiently with your little ones, and answer *all* their endless questionings. Do not rashly check the rising spirit of free inquiry with an impatient word or frown. Says the poet:

"Answer all a child's questions, and ask others as simple
As its own, yet wisely framed
To waken and prove the young child's faculties,
As though its mind was some sweet instrument,
And you with breath and touch were finding out
What stops and keys would yield the sweetest music."

Now, I will freely acknowledge—1. That attention, such as we want to get from children, is a very difficult thing for anybody to give. The incidents of yesterday and the cares of to-day and business and pleasures of to-morrow, will divert and scatter attention. 2. That fixed attention to religious subjects is particularly hard for any one, and *especially* hard for children to give; but hard as it is, *we must have it*, and no half-hearted, languid attention either, if we are to do any real good in the Sunday-school. 3. Says an old writer to Sunday-school teachers: "Let me tell you, you will not get it by claiming it; by demanding it as a right; or entreating it as a favor, by urging upon your pupils the importance of the subject, the sacredness of the day, the kindness of the teachers, or the great and solemn character of the truths which you have to impart. All these are legitimate arguments to be used with older Christians, but will not do to rely upon with children. Nothing in the long run—except fear, which is a very unsatisfactory motive—can keep a child's attention fixed but a sense of *real interest* in the things which you are saying. The subject must claim attention for itself, and therefore, the teacher needs always to be accurately prepared and well furnished with correct knowledge, parallel passages, illustrations, facts, anecdotes, definitions of hard words, allusions, poetry, etc. In all your teaching, forget not to recall the fresh spirit of your childhood in all its warmth and earnestness, remembering that he is the wisest teacher who can combine the man's intellect with the child's heart."

Now it may be, after all, teacher, that your children may be inattentive, or they will disobey your commands, or they will fail to treat you with respect; but if that should be so, we will reply, in conclusion, in the impressive words of Mr. Fitch: "Ask yourself in that case whether your own behavior is uniform and dignified; whether you ever give commands without seeing that they are obeyed; whether you waste your words or your influence in an injudicious way; whether there is anything in your conduct that reveals to the children a want of punctuality or order, or of earnestness or steadfastness on your part? For children are very keen observers of character, and, in the long run, are sure to feel loyalty and affection for one who is manifestly anxious to do them good, and who can be uniformly relied on in word and in deed."

XVIII.

THE ART OF QUESTIONING.

HERE is a real *art* in knowing where, when, and how to put a good question, that shall quicken the memory, set the mind to thinking, and call back the reflective faculties. Such are the possibilities of a question. A large proportion of all the good teaching in our Sabbath-schools is brought about by the simple process of questions and answers. "A question unveils the soul. Nothing can escape a question. A question reveals decision." Hence the skill required. Mr. J. G. Fitch says: "The success and efficiency of our teaching depend more on the skill and judgment with which we put questions than on any other single circumstance."

This art is to be learned, like any other art, by much study and patient practice, for we best learn the art of questioning *by questioning*. Augustine says: "A boy can preach, but a man only can catechise," and Lord Bacon says: "A wise question is the half of knowledge." Therefore the great skill in teaching consists mainly in the right forming and asking of questions.

If this be true, it follows that this subject should be regarded as of special importance by every teacher. Teachers often say that they cannot succeed in asking questions without the book; that they do not know what to ask. To this I reply, 1. There is never any difficulty in forming the question where there is an interest to obtain the answer. 2. It is generally unwise to ask any question unless we have an interest in obtaining the answer. Do not tantalize the little ones. Says Mr. Hassell: "A question under some circumstances will merely produce an exercise of the memory; under others an exercise of reasoning; and under others again it will stimulate inquiry," and we may add, awaken curiosity. Mr. Groser says: "The true scope of questioning-power is as follows: To awaken curiosity or the desire to know; to arouse the memory or the recollection of what is already known; or to point out something unknown, which may be inferred from that which is known." A question skillfully put will arouse, will fix attention, concentrate the thoughts, and so discipline the mind of the pupil.

There are, however, many bad and indifferent questions put, in religious teaching, which a little knowledge of the correct rules of the art of questioning will enable us to avoid. Frequently a slight variation in the form changes a bad question into a good one. For instance: "Moses was a good man, was he not?" is a bad question. "What kind of a man was Moses?" is a good question, as it awakens thought. "What do you understand by faith and repentance?" is a bad question, for it is ambiguous and indefinite, and perplexes the child. "Will you tell me what is faith?" is a good question, for it compels the child to think and to inquire—it puts into his hand the laboring oar and he must row. "Did David kill Goliath with a stone or with a sword?" This is a bad question. It is involved and suggestive. Ask the child simply, "With what did David kill Goliath?" and the question is a good one, in strict conformity with the laws of questioning and of the child-mind.

Another class of questions is very common, but well nigh useless, namely, leading questions, such as, "Was David a good man?" "Was Goliath a wicked man?" These are mostly bad or indifferent questions, and are almost a total loss to the teacher. Slightly vary them in the following way, and you make them at once, in every aspect, good questions. "What kind of a man was David?" "What kind of a man was Goliath?" Teachers will remember, therefore, to avoid ambiguous or indefinite, involved or suggestive, and leading questions, which latter are answered "Yes" or "No," for they are generally of little avail.

What kind of questions, then, shall Sabbath-school teachers seek to use? I reply:

1. Questions of *Examination*, in order to find

out what the pupil already knows; to gauge his present knowledge, and ascertain what he needs to know.

2. Questions of *explanation* of particular words, which should be put freely while reading the lesson.

3. Questions of *actual instruction*, or reflective questions, thus making the pupil teach himself, or find out as much as possible by thinking and inquiring, and thus leading him to correct his own answers. Much instruction may be communicated by asking questions and correcting the answers, but great care should be taken to make the most of the answers, and to do full justice to them. Socrates's plan was to lead the pupil by a pleasant question to discover his own error, instead of directly charging him with it. Encourage your scholars by all means to ask questions with freedom, and give your teaching more the form of an earnest conversation.

4. Questions of *recapitulation* or review. In this way you ascertain whether your lessons are received, for the test is their telling it back to you in their own language. You question the lesson *into* the minds of the scholars, and then question it *out* again. Herbert, in his "Country Parson," gives us an illustration. After asking, "Since man is so miserable, what is to be done?" and the answerer could not tell, instead of telling him, he properly asked the following simple question, "What would he do if he were in a ditch?" This familiar illustra-

tion made the answer so plain that he was even ashamed of his ignorance; for he could not but say, "He would make haste out of it as fast as he could." Then he proceeded to ask whether he could get out of the ditch alone or whether he needed a helper, and who was that helper? This is the skill; and doubtless the Holy Scripture intends thus much when it condescends to the naming of a plough, leaven, boys piping and dancing, showing that ordinary things are to be washed and cleansed, and serve as lights for heavenly truths.

5. Questions with an *ellipsis* are most useful in the review or summing up of the lesson, as, "He says, I am the good—*Shepherd*. Come unto—*me*," etc.

6. Questions may often be used to kindle the reflective faculties, to exercise the mind and to develope ideas.

7. And, lastly, questions *applying* divine truth—softly, thoughtfully, and in a few words—should never be forgotten. Jesus did so and so. "*Do you?*" David said, "Oh how love I thy law?" "*Do you so love it?*" Solomon said, "Remember now thy Creator." Charlie, "*Do you love to remember your Creator?*" or "*Why not?*" etc.

Not only are the character and adaptation of the question of great importance, but the manner and look of the eye and the tone of voice and the manner of receiving the answer. The manner should be kind, gentle, life-like, and winning; the look of the eye should beam with life and interest, while the tone of voice should bespeak great tenderness and sympathy. A cold, formal tone of voice will repel the answer, even with a good question. It should be sprightly, and respectfully familiar and natural. Children cannot endure coldness nor dullness nor dryness; therefore avoid all long pauses and sluggish manner and heavy voice. The way which you receive the answers will determine the question whether your scholars will freely answer you or not. Make the most of an answer unless it is absolutely wrong, and if wrong, say, "Will some scholar tell me why that answer is wrong?" Search out for all the points or hints of truth you can find in the answer of the child, and unfold it and hold it up in the most favorable and gracious light.

Never snap up a scholar, or neglect or ridicule his answers, however faulty. Always be candid and sincere, and your scholars will soon learn to trust themselves with you. A sharp, harsh reply will close the lips of a whole class. Enunciate every word with clearness. Vary the questions with all patience if not answered readily, and never think a child does not know because he does not answer the question at once. Be sure "never to tell a child what you could make that child tell you."

Let your questions have a regular connection, so that one will naturally follow another, and in fact, glide into the next, and "say as little as you can in questioning and teaching, but so say it as to cause the children to say as much as possible."

Then again be careful to adapt your questions well. Do not tell much in your questions. Put the right question to the right scholar, for it will not do to ask A or B or C a question which only D in the class can answer, for we are not to ask any child any question unless we suppose the answer is in the mind of the child.

It is of particular importance that in the commencement of a lesson we always start aright. Have some easy, pleasant questions ready, which they will be glad to answer. No matter what occurs, never manifest impatience or severity, or descend to a witticism or a sneer. A sneering, sarcastic teacher should be left out of the school. Therefore gladly receive and develope, in the most charitable manner, the half-uttered, stammering answer of the child at your feet, and your children, in their hearts, will bless you.

Dr. Arnold, the great teacher at Rugby, said: "It was his practice to teach by questioning, and as a general rule, he never gave information except as a kind of reward for an answer. His explanations were as short as possible, and his questions were of a kind to call the attention of the boys to the real point of every subject, and to disclose to them the exact boundaries of what they knew and what they did not know." Let me add to this Archdeacon Bather's account of how he became a catechist. He says in his "Hints on Catechising:"

"Perhaps, gentle reader, before I actually enter

upon my task of teaching you to teach others by catechising, it may be as well to tell you how I became a catechist myself; for the thought seized upon me and occupied me much in very early life. I was at school at Rugby, and at the time I speak of, was in what we called the '*upper third*.' The '*upper fourth*' was under the care of Mr. Innes, afterwards Head Master of the Royal Free Grammar School at Warwick. As I was sitting one evening in the room of my private tutor, Mr. Homer, some one knocked at the door, and in came Mr. Innes. 'Bather,' says he, 'when Mr. Homer has done with you, will you come up into my room? I want to speak to you; you will find nobody there but O—— (naming one of my school-fellows) and myself.' Of course I went; and Mr. Innes, motioning my companion to a chair and myself to another, took his own and addressed us thus: 'I am going to set you two boys very hard at work. Pray, O——, do you know anything about astronomy?' 'Not much, I am afraid, sir.' 'And you, Bather?' 'Not so much as O——, I am afraid.' 'Well, now, do not flatter yourselves that I am going to tell you anything about it, for I shall do no such thing. Nevertheless, you shall know more about it, and a good deal, too, before you go out of this room.' He then put questions to us both, by which he soon elicited all the particulars of such little knowledge as we possessed; and then he questioned us further, soon causing us to make many blunders, and then making us correct our answers, so that we certainly did quit the room with fuller and more orderly notions of the matter than we brought into it." He says, although this did not make him an astronomer, yet it led him to think and discern what must be the most effectual way of imparting knowledge, for "under Mr. Innes his interest never flagged; he could have listened all night."

From the same source is here added another illustration of teaching by the means of leading questions. "Then was Jesus led up of the Spirit into the wilderness," etc. "Then was Jesus." What do you mean by "then was Jesus?" (Hesitates.) "Then took Mary a pound of ointment." What do you mean by "then took Mary?" Then Mary took. What do you mean by "then was Jesus?" and the answer came readily, "Then Jesus was." Now you shall question me. Put me a question to which each clause shall be a reply, beginning with the first. "When was Jesus led up to be tempted?" "Then." So here you are taught—what? The time when these things took place. Put me a question to which the words "led up" shall be an answer. "What was done to Jesus?" He was "led up." Put a question for the word "Spirit." "Who led him up?" "The Spirit." So of the word "wilderness." "Whither did the Spirit lead him?" "Into the wilderness."

Let us add one more illustration, showing how to put questions to help and lead. The manner must, of course, be right, for a clumsy method will hinder rather than help, and if we expect a right answer the question must be a simple one, or one that will not admit of being put as *two* questions. The following anecdote may serve as the illustration: "A lady came one day to my school and requested me to let her hear the children catechised. The class happened to be reading the third chapter of the Acts, the first of which reads thus: "Now Peter and John went up together into the temple at the hour of prayer, being the ninth honr.' 'Well,' I said to the teacher, 'stop there and question them on that verse.' 'At what time of day?' said he, 'did those things take place which are here set down?' 'At the ninth hour,' replied the class. But then a poor boy became a little frightened at something or other, and consequently puzzled; and after some hesitation said, 'Well, then, at the ninth hour, *who went where?*' The first boy in the class smiled a little, but made no answer; the next seemed to think a little, but still no voice came. I took care that nobody should answer out of his turn, and the question was put to every boy severally to the bottom of the class. The lady turned to me and expressed her surprise that out of a class of five-and-twenty boys nobody could answer. 'Well, ma'am, I am afraid you will consider these five-and-twenty boys very stupid, but let us look a little further into the matter.' And then, turning round, my eye caught that of Jack Thompson. 'Jack,' said I, 'how many stupid boys have we got in our second class?' 'One, sir,' says Jack. 'And who may he be?' 'The teacher, sir.' 'You must prove your words, Jack: come and teach the class yourself.' Now Jack was not an impudent boy; but as he advanced and saw the lady looking at him, he did not appear so confused as poor Peter had done before, and he betook himself at once to business. 'You have told us,' said he, 'that the things related in this verse took place at the ninth hour of the day; to what was that hour wont to be devoted?' 'To prayer.' 'And what was the building called that was open, at that time, to receive the worshippers?' 'The temple.' 'Are not some persons specially mentioned who came to the temple at that time?' 'Yes.' 'How many?' 'Two.' 'What were their names?' 'Peter and John.' 'Where did Peter and John go at the ninth hour?' 'Into the temple.' 'What for?' 'To pray,' etc. The lady began to perceive that the children did know something about the matter, and Jack Thompson, being concerned for the conduct of his class, proceeded to ask them a great many more questions, to which the answers were very satisfactory. The lady good-humoredly expressed her approval, and I said, 'Now, madam, you see that all that was the matter was, that poor Peter, being a little confused, put his questions in a clumsy manner. Depend upon it, he will not soon do the like again.'"

Questions should be progressive, that is, they should proceed from the simple and the known to the faintly known, and thence to the unknown.

XIX.

THE TEACHERS' MEETING.

 REGULAR weekly meeting of Sabbath-school teachers for conference and prayer about all school matters, and a mutual contribution of thoughts and illustrations and plans of teaching adapted to each and to all the various classes on the next Sabbath's lesson, is now considered an indispensable necessity. And it is a great social and religious privilege as well.

We are all unworthy, and need to learn how to teach Scripture truths attractively to youthful minds. All need training for the work, and the weekly teachers' meetings ought to be the grand normal training-schools for Sabbath-school teachers everywhere. Every Sabbath-school ought also to have a Bible-class or two for the training of teachers. The almost half a million of Sabbath-school teachers in our land—the *masses*—cannot mingle with us in council in our great Conventions and Institutes, and consequently the few favored ones must imbibe the spirit and avail themselves of ample materials, and carry it down to the quiet, devoted workers in common Sabbath-schools through the means of a well-ordered teachers' meeting. The meeting can be held for one hour and a half on a week-day evening at the lecture-room, or, better yet, at the superintendent's house or that of one of the teachers, alternately. It is conducted usually by the superintendent, but sometimes by the pastor, or by one of the teachers who can sustain the interest.

But we are met at this point with a stubborn and overwhelming fact, viz.: a large proportion of all these meetings attempted to be held have resulted in a failure, and have been abandoned, so that now in some places not one school in ten or twenty holds such a meeting. With such an experience we can never ask Sabbath-school teachers to try the experiment on the old plan. We must count the cost, and Sabbath-school men, with only an hour or two in a week for it, cannot afford to make mistakes or failures. Time is too precious.

The great practical question arises, What are the causes of failure? Is it anything inherent in these meetings? or is it in the wrong mode of conducting them? After a most careful investigation of the subject, especially during the last fifteen or twenty years, I have come to the deliberate conclusion that it is owing almost entirely to the wrong plans on which they are conducted. What have been these wrong plans?

1st. They have ordinarily been conducted on the Bible-class, question-book, commentary-studying, and theological-discussing plans; and on those plans they have, and will, in at least nine cases out of ten, result in failure, whether in the hands of pastors or of superintendents. Teachers do not gain enough in such meetings to reward them for their time and trouble in coming, and consequently they cannot be censured for non-attendance.

2d. Another plan of conducting them is in the form of lectures. But on this plan not even an expository lecture has prevented the meeting from being a failure. Occasionally a pastor or a superintendent, with great expository powers and a sprightly manner of analyzing truth and a personal sympathy with the teachers and children, can sustain and make these meetings interesting and profitable on this plan, and to such we can say—God bless you—*go on!* But we cannot afford to recommend any plan for general adoption with such a prospect of failure.

What, then, must be done? We say decidedly, *revolutionize your plans*, and meet with the direct aim and purpose *of helping one another* in your work, and especially on the next Sabbath's lesson.

What then are the objects of teachers' meetings, and how should they be conducted? The objects appear to me to be—1. To get all the teachers well acquainted, socially and religiously, and as teachers. 2. To combine our mutual confidences, sympathies and prayers. 3. To mutually help each other and relieve each other's difficulties by conferring together on such questions as—how best to secure and retain attention;—how to question; —how to prepare the lesson and present it, and teach it;—how to draw lessons of instruction, illustrate and apply truth;—how to analyze the lesson, lay out the plan of it, and break it up into small, convenient parcels, adapted to all capacities from the infant up to the adult classes;—how to make the Word of God most useful, most interesting and most impressive to youthful minds, convicting of sin and converting to God; and the thorough training of the young in the Christian life, and in the sound knowledge of revealed truth.

The way to conduct these meetings is, to go to work naturally, systematically and directly, in a common-sense way, to accomplish these grand objects. Suppose, after singing two verses of an appropriate hymn, a direct prayer of two or three minutes, and one verse of Scripture that just meets the case, the leader inquires for the next half hour the size, regularity, etc., of the different classes, and asks counsel to correct irregularities. In this way the teachers will become so well acquainted with each other's classes that they can intelligently pray for each other. Then have a recess of ten or fifteen minutes for introduction and social intercourse; after which another half hour should be devoted to inquiring of each teacher for the various *best thoughts* of the lesson for them to use. Let the next meeting be directed to the difficulties, and how to relieve them, and the last half hour to asking for illustrations for the week or month's lesson. At the next meeting inquire, Have you *visited* your scholars during the month, and what have you found of interest in your visits? Then devote the last half hour to examples and *plans of teaching* different verses by several teachers. At the fourth and last meeting of the month inquire, Is there any special religious interest in your class? or, Why not? and lastly, How can you *apply* the lesson so as best to make a saving impression?

In some such way I would meet real present wants, avoiding routine, and providing something fresh and varied at every meeting, just adapted to all. In some such way conduct your meetings, and no teacher can afford to be absent.

In a country school district Sabbath-school let the teachers turn all their sociability into this channel, and set apart, say Thursday evening of each week, for a pleasant social teachers' meeting at the residence of the superintendent or one of the teachers, alternating about. Let the farmers arrange to leave their work an hour earlier on that evening for the sake of the great blessing to their children. Provide attendants for the lady teachers. Suppose the superintendent lives one mile north of the school-house, and two teachers are one mile east, three south, and four west. The two young lady teachers "one mile east" have no escort, but the superintendent remembers that in the next house further east, the only son of Esquire Jones, a fine young man of sixteen years, has just drifted out of the Sabbath-school, and is inclining toward fast horses and gay companions. The superintendent yearns to reach and save him. He thinks and prays over the matter until he feels deeply for the youth. He then visits him, and approaches him with unusual respect—informs him that he has come to ask a particular favor—will he accept the post of librarian in our flourishing little Sabbath-school? He readily consents. The superintendent then says, "Charlie, we teachers have a delightful social gathering at each other's houses every Thursday evening, and as you have a fine horse and buggy, cannot you make it convenient to bring up the two Misses S—— to that meeting?" Why, of course, it is just what the superintendent wants, and it is also just what Charlie wants—something to do, and soon, by God's grace, Charlie becomes a true Christian.

In whatever form the teachers' meetings are conducted it is indispensable—1. That the conductor feels a sincere respect for each teacher, and treats his opinions with candor. 2. That the conductor shall adapt his questions to each individual, and ask those questions with real courtesy and consideration. 3. It is absolutely necessary that the conductor should receive all replies in a life-like manner, with due respect, and make the best of them. If the answers are not well received, it will close the lips of the teachers. They must draw together, and a dull, prosy conductor will check them all.

There is great value in the combined counsels and

experience of almost any common band of teachers if fairly and fully drawn out. It will often be seen that "the commonest mind has thoughts worthy of the rarest." In this way the teachers' meetings can be sustained in the hands of ordinary superintendents, and will become the most attractive gatherings in the whole community. An accomplished young lady said to me: "One such meeting as this is worth more than a dozen costly New York parties." The teachers will regularly attend, for they need the assistance which can here be obtained. As well ask a brakeman to run a locomotive, or a spinner to superintend a factory, or an untaught man to teach an academy, as to ask an inexperienced person, or even a classical scholar, to teach divine truth when no one has taught him how. James Gall says, most truly, "Education is the highest of all the sciences, and teaching the most important of all the arts." Teachers then, need training, and the teachers' meeting can be made one of the most valuable means of securing it. One of the great objects of Sabbath-School Teachers' Institutes is to train superintendents, teachers, etc., so that they can interestingly and profitably conduct their weekly teachers' meetings, which are the real institutes for the great mass of teachers.

Examples.

The following Examples are real, as taken from my note-book during the present year:

I. At one time the lesson was the parable of the Prodigal

Son. The first teacher was called up for the best thought for his class in the lesson. He replied, "Like the prodigal, all children want to have their own way." The second teacher, "The farther he wandered the greater his misery." The third, "When *starving*, came to himself." 4. He resolved to "arise and go to his father." 5. "He *returned*." 6. "After his father fell on his neck, he *confessed*." 7. "His confidence in his father when he returned." 8. "His father saw him a *great way off*." 9. "Father *ran*,"—old men do not usually run. 10. "With joy *embraced* and kissed him," etc. 11. "The degradation of a sinful course." 12. The father's wonderful condescension and willingness.

II. At another teachers' meeting the lesson was Luke xviii. 18–27. The Young Ruler.—First, prayer, singing, and reading of the lesson. Then called on the teachers for their plan of teaching the lesson.

The *First Teacher* gave five heads. 1. Question, "What shall I do?" 2. Knowing the law. 3. Taking up the cross. 4. Rejecting the cross. 5. The great obstacle.

Second Teacher.—1. Eternal life, what is it? 2. Have you kept the law? 3. What else was required? 4. Come. 5. Overcome every obstacle. 6. You must love nothing better than Christ.

Third Teacher's plan was—The Young Ruler was, 1. Rich; 2. Pleasing; 3. Respectful; 4. Ready to learn; 5. Prostrate—the custom of the country; 6. Put first his love to neighbors; 7. Commandments—Pharisee. Show the children how far they can go and yet be lost. He was a church member, an officer in the church, a ruler: he came to Jesus prostrate, prayed respectfully—Jesus applied the touchstone and *all* was *wanting*.

Fourth Teacher.—1. Young man's great desire. 2. It was to be saved. 3. Go to God's word. 4. Justified himself. 5. He loved money more than he loved God. 6. Hollow-hearted. Study the scholar as much as the lesson.

Fifth Teacher.—1. Young man's question and manner. 2. Asserting he kept all the law. 3. He thought himself honest and sincere, but was deceived. 4. Wanted satisfying peace. 5. Not willing to remove his idols. 6. Great ignorance of the young man. 7. Riches a great hindrance. 8. See our Lord's firmness.

Sixth Teacher.—We must show our love to Christ by love to our neighbors.

Seventh Teacher.—With man it is impossible, but not with God.

Eighth Teacher.—Something must be given up for Christ. What? Pride, sloth, ill-temper, bad company, bad books, love of dress, pleasure.—See Abraham going to a strange land. Offering Isaac, etc.

Ninth Teacher.—Ruler had his ideas of *doing* something to gain heaven, and was at work for it. The great Teacher took him on his own ground and *convicted* him of *sin.*

Tenth Teacher.—A child says: "Why, here is an honest, sincere seeker, who went to Jesus in the right manner and way, but failed." How hard to be saved! But see—1. His question. 2. The Saviour's answer. 3. The obstacles and hindrances. 4. The greatest apparent defect is in the second table of the law. If perfectly convicted, why so confident? etc.

III. Lesson, Matthew viii. 1–4. Have eight distinct exercises. 1. Read the lesson. 2. Catechise or question upon it. 3. The numerical exercise or asking, How many things, etc. 4. *Explanations* and illustrations of difficult words. 5. Draw out great important *thoughts* of the lesson. 6. Call forth the *lessons* of instruction. 7. Make the *application* to heart and life. 8. Review of the whole; and then, if desired, two more exercises can be added by turning the lesson into *prayer*, and next to a *paraphrase* formed of the verses.

There are *three* kinds of teaching. 1. Catechising or questioning. 2. Conversational. 3. Lecturing. Which is yours? We might add a fourth; but that is not teaching at all, only it is sometimes called so—viz., Reading questions from a question-book, and reading the answers. Good teaching is earnest, hearty work.

IV. The fourth and last example is of the social form of teachers' meeting. I give the notes of one held on the evening of December 11, 1867. We met at 6 o'clock P. M., precisely, at the house of Mr. C——; opened with singing and prayer. Then had half an hour's studying of the lesson, which was upon the Atonement. Some of the thoughts drawn out were: Mediation,—arbitration,—the God-man,—dead goat and the goat sent away,—the passover,—the victim,—a substitute,—altar, victim, shed blood; vivid picture of offering the lamb;—atonement looks both ways;—blood cleanseth. How do you get the atonement? Have you got it? How do you prove gratitude to God for it? Exalting the great truth, "Christ died for me." He is the only barrier against eternal death. The lesson was shown in three phases: 1. The Redeemer buys us from sin—is our ransom; 2. Saves us from sin; 3. Reconciles us to God. Take first under three heads: 1. Man is a ruined wanderer; 2. Man a captive; 3. Man is free in Christ and saved. After the lesson was thus considered, the next half hour was devoted to *business*. The library, Christmas exercises, singing, and length of opening exercises, and the treasury, were topics. The next hour was given to tea and social intercourse. The last hour was devoted to accounts of interesting or discouraging things in the teachers' classes, and work, and intermingled with frequent prayer and singing. All was conducted spiritually and in earnest, and it was a precious three hours.

XX.

VISITING THE SCHOLARS.

VERY Sabbath-school teacher should regularly visit his scholars once a month, and every Sabbath-school superintendent should visit his teachers regularly once in three months. These are very important and yet too often neglected duties. A superintendent can hardly discharge his duties to the teachers without frequently visiting them. This should be no mere formal visit. It should be a Christian conference about all the details, particularly of their classes and their duties. The superintendent is the regular counsellor and guide of the teachers. He should talk about their teaching, about each and all their scholars, their difficulties, their trials and successes, and aid and encourage them by every means. These visits should be made so cheerful and pleasant, so free from fault-finding and complaint, that the teachers will hail them with great joy.

The Sabbath-school teacher also, from his own necessities and from duty, must needs visit his scholars often. He has a real errand to the home of every child. He can snatch intervals of time going to or returning from business. He cannot teach that child aright and to good advantage unless he is well acquainted with all his home influences; with all there is in the child's surroundings to help or hinder the teacher's work; with all the dangers, temptations, and trials of the child's everyday life; with all the characteristics of parents and friends. It is from the vicinity of these homes that the teacher will be enabled to see and hear things that will furnish him with good illustrations. He can obtain the parents' co-operation and friendship, and have personal interviews and gain the child's spiritual confidence in these visits to its home and fireside circle. "My teacher has come to see *me*," is often the joyful utterance of the grateful little ones.

Sabbath-school teachers should never neglect this privilege, neither should they make careless or indifferent visits. Arouse up and think your visit all out beforehand. Think what in substance you are going to talk about, what you ought to say, so as to make your visit as welcome and as profitable as possible both to parents and scholars. Have an errand to every house. Carry some little book or tract or paper, if convenient. Give them some interesting and valuable information, or make earnest inquiries and give good wishes and prayers for rich blessings, temporal and spiritual. Choose the right time and seek favorable opportunities. Absentees must, of course, be visited without delay, for it may be sickness has detained them. "The sickness of a child is a golden opportunity for the teacher; God himself ploughs the ground and he must not withhold the seed." Especially avail yourself of seasons when the heart is made tender by illness, afflictions, and trials. Then be constant and true, for it may be your harvest-time of souls. "Oh, to be the guiding star of such a little circle is one of the highest privileges of earth." Teacher, may that privilege and blessing be yours.

We add a single illustrative example from "*The Teacher Teaching*:"

"A decently-dressed woman calls at your house and begs for a shawl to protect a neighbor of hers from the cold when she goes out to her daily work. You have a shawl. You have laid it aside for this very purpose. Why not give it to her and have done with it? If you do not know the person who calls, it would be very injudicious to entrust to a stranger what you intended for a third person. It may be pawned for strong drink, or retained by one who is not in want. Better go or send and satisfy yourself that the need exists, and see that it is supplied. You wisely conclude to look for yourself. You find the object of your charity, and ascertain that she is a superior needle-woman, capable of earning her living, but not able to find work where there is none. If she could hire a room in some part of the city nearer the demand for work, she might succeed. You give her the shawl, and with it a few words of encouragement. In a day or two you are at a meeting of the directors of the Industrial Home or Orphans' Society, and allude to the case of this woman. A young lady present immediately recollects a poor woman, whom she has seen during the week, who has a room to rent, and perhaps it would exactly suit. The parties are brought together and the room is taken. Two wants are thus promptly supplied—the want of a *room* and the want of a *tenant*. But how came the young lady to know of such a room? Why, simply by visiting the mother of one of her class in the Sunday-school. It was not any part of her plan to obtain any such information; nor could she have known that it might be of any advantage to her or to any one else for her to possess it. The indirect result of this simple visit accomplished—what? 1. It secured a tenant for a vacant room, and thus helped a poor woman to pay her rent. 2. It put another poor woman in a comfortable and convenient position to earn her own living. 3. It laid the mother of one of her Sunday-school children under great obligation to her, and thus increased her influence and her power to do good both to mother and child. It will take a strong force to sunder that tie. 4. It brought to the new tenant Christian care and sympathy, which she before lacked, and the way for her attendance on the stated means of grace."

Thus is exemplified, by a single real and comparatively unimportant incident in humble life, the power of the Sunday-school machinery, in its legitimate movements, to improve and elevate social condition and character. It was all the work of that little wheel in our machinery called VISITING.

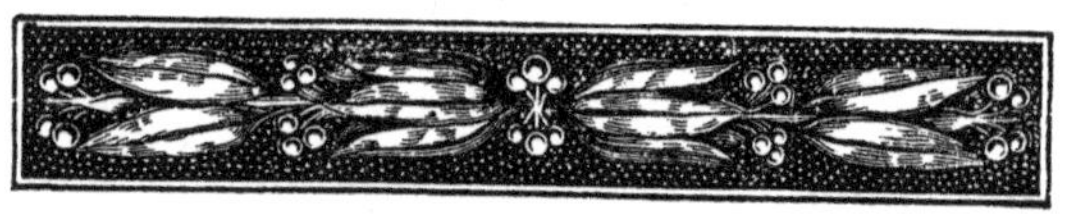

XXI.

SYSTEMATIC DISTRICT CHRISTIAN VISITATION.

HE plan here given in its present form grew out of an exigency in the operations of the Missionary Committee of the New York Sunday-School Union in the summer of 1856.

In their great endeavor to reach the neglected masses of children and youth, more than sixty thousand seemed to be beyond their reach. A more *thorough* work was needed. Occasional visits and ordinary attention did not so gain the acquaintance and confidence as to rescue these neglected ones. They were the most destitute and needy, and the most important to reach in our city. After much consideration and prayer, this plan was adopted, presented to, and accepted by the churches in New York and Brooklyn, and it was soon adopted by other cities and States also. Everywhere it has developed astonishing results, increasing Sabbath-schools and churches, and speedily transforming dark neighborhoods.

Forty-four churches of various evangelical denominations entered upon the work within a few months after its introduction, and quite uniformly the Sabbath-schools *doubled* their scholars within the first month or two, and in some marked instances church members and congregations were more than doubled in numbers within six months. As long as it was faithfully worked it everywhere prospered, demonstrating that the plan was a good one.

It is based on the great command, "*Go ye and teach.*" It believes that every church-member should be a working Christian, a real missionary; that "every man should *speak to his neighbor, and each one to his brother;*" that every Christian's business should be so arranged as to give a wider scope for his religion, that he may become, in a degree, a voluntary missionary. It proposes to *systematize* the work. Mere voluntary personal effort is at times so fitful and evanescent as not to be sufficiently reliable.

The plan is for every church to take a definite district as its special missionary field—in the city a certain number of blocks and streets, and in the country a number of miles square, or neighborhoods, properly arranged so as to give every other church a portion of the field to work.

All this is to be subdivided by a committee of the church into small sub-sections of from five to fifteen families, proportionate to the number of able members. A sub-section is assigned to the member, and becomes his or her little parish, on which to bestow especial labor, sympathy, and prayers. He is to

visit it every month, invite all the children to some Sunday-school, the family to church, supply with the Bible, tract, etc., and do all possible temporal and spiritual good. Once a month each church devotes one of the weekly prayer-meetings to hearing reports from the visitors, and conferring and praying over this great work. Special care is taken not to proselyte; not to take a child from one school to another, or induce a person to leave one church for another, but to respect the rights of all. Individuals are not considered under any obligations to *confine* their visits to their assigned districts, but still enjoy the Christian liberty of going everywhere and doing good to all men as they have opportunity.

This work is—1. A holy work. 2. A deliberate work. 3. It is a work of pure good-will. 4. Says Rev. Dr. Chalmers: "No other ministration is to be offered than that of respect and kindness." 5. They are to go just so far "as they will be gratefully met by the population." 6. Visit rich and poor, but carefully select districts adapted to the visitors. 7. Seek the confidence of parents and children; be patient, be persevering, be courageous, be sympathetic, and take no notice of repulses. 8. Enter no house in vain. Leave some kind suggestion, counsel, or sympathy in regard to spiritual or temporal interests. 9. Relieve all want and distress possible; inculcate temperance, cleanliness, and economy. 10. Counsel with mothers with reference to their children. 11. Give a fraternal aspect to your

visits, and avoid controversy, and generally even argument.

If each professing Christian in our churches who is able would become responsible for the regular visitation of but four neglected families, every family in our land would be faithfully visited. "What a plain, simple, magnificent idea is here presented!" A regular Christian army of occupation for our whole country. Says the Rev. Dr. Guthrie: "It would everywhere bring life into contact with death, and cover the whole outlying population, even as the prophet with his own body covered the dead body of the child." The motto is: EVERY CHILD IN THE SABBATH-SCHOOL, AND EVERY FAMILY IN THE CHURCH.

XXII.

NEW MISSION-SCHOOLS.

IN all our great cities, in the town and country, there are vast numbers of immortal youth far beyond the reach of churches and church Sabbath-schools, and therefore, it becomes necessary to carry the Sunday-school to them. A room is obtained, conveniently located, with seats, books, etc. The children are gathered, taught to read, to sing, to pray, presented with library books, papers, etc., and thus innumerable blessings are sent down into destitute families, and soon, like leaven, the Gospel is seen diffusing itself everywhere among the mass.

Something like seventy of these mission-schools are now successfully sustained in New York City alone, with twelve to fifteen thousand pupils in them. Roman Catholic, Jewish, and other classes of children are in this way easily and successfully reached, and permanently benefited. This instrumentality must be largely increased everywhere. Some five or six different denominations often unite in the labors of one of these schools, and all work together in the most beautiful harmony. This movement is in the highest sympathy with that *aggressive* feature of the system, before named.

But to come to the details of this work, and how it should be begun and carried on: First choose wisely the location for a new church or mission Sabbath-school. Then select one or more men and women full of life and zeal as a nucleus of interest and labor. Next survey and visit systematically all the families in the district, and present the objects and the value and adaptedness of the Sunday-school to their wants. Pray much and at every step, privately and socially, especially in the early stages of the effort.

Get all ready for a good commencement. Have every thing arranged, so that not a moment of delay in finding the right hymn, or in singing it, will prompt the children to find something else to do. Do not admit children faster than you can conveniently control them. Some superintendents aim at gathering a rush of scholars the first Sabbath or two, and the result is that they lose months in getting to order and control of the children. It is often better to admit only a dozen or two new scholars at a time, and get them well classified and arranged, and in the hands of good teachers. There must be order, and the superintendent must wait for it, although he may not at the first do much beside. Much depends upon starting right. Have Testaments, hymn-books, and Sunday-school papers, if possible, ready on the first Sabbath.

Select a clear, distinct, easy lesson at the first, and whatever is done, let it be well done. Select the teachers carefully, and admit none who have not a good report, and are not of a teachable spirit. Meet with the teachers socially every week, if possible, to aid them with your suggestions and help. Be cheerful, earnest, and respectful to all. Keep up a regular visitation of teachers and scholars, and let your visits bear a fraternal and not an inquisitorial aspect. Prove yourselves the true friends of parents and scholars, and never get out of patience or discouraged because you cannot gain the children of Roman Catholics or Jewish parents at once: it may be only a question of time. At any rate, do them all the good you can at their homes, whether you ever lead them to the Sunday-school or not. Duty is ours—results belong to God. Through the children reach the parents, and through the parents reach the children. Let your errand to the house always be one of kindness and good-will, so that if they do not receive you kindly it will be because they misunderstand you. These visits, however, are almost invariably well received if made in a natural, pleasant manner, proceeding from a "charity which hopeth all things." Respect and honor the parents all you can, whether they commit their children to your care or not. Exhibit our beautiful library books, our sweet songs, our attractive children's papers, and speak of the great kindness and love of the teachers to the children.

It is very desirable to have a course of regular

week-day evening lectures for the children and parents. One week it may be "Jerusalem," another "coal," another "coral," and the next "the ocean," and then some subject of natural history, as the "elephant;" and illustrate highly to meet the eyes. Take especial care of the older boys and girls, and strive to introduce week-day exercises that will interest and please them. Appoint them upon committees and to little offices, and give them all something to do—something that they can do, something that they will do cheerfully.

The following, from *The Sunday-School Times*, is a beautiful illustrative example of mission Sunday-school work and teaching. It is entitled "Bill Jones; or, Our Colored Sabbath-school:"

It was one of those perfect Sabbaths in the early June, that I walked with trembling heart along the locust-shadowed sidewalk leading to our little chapel. On that day our colored Sunday-school was to be organized; and we, who only a few weeks since had professed before men and angels to love our Saviour, were to be enlisted as workers in our Master's vineyard.

What can be done to improve the religious condition of our colored population? was a question which had long occasioned anxious thought among the godly of our village. Originally slaves, they had, when the law of liberation was proclaimed through New York, refused to remove farther than the grassy common, where, almost within the shadow of "Massa's house," they were allowed to build their humble cabins. Increased afterward in numbers, the suburbs of the town had become edged with their miserable tenements. One or two attempts had been made to establish preaching among them by a minister of their own race, but thus far without success. True, in the "brick church," a part of the gallery was set apart especially for their use. Still the "dark corner" (as the mischievous boys called it) was only occupied by a few old uncles and aunties, while the rest, though within sound of the sweetest of all Sabbath bells, were as utterly without God in the world as their brethren in Africa.

At length a Sabbath-school was determined on. As most of those able and willing to work were already engaged, one of the officers of the church volunteered to superintend the school, provided he might have the assistance of a band of young girls, who hitherto had been privileged to assemble week after week as a Bible-class in the "pastor's study."

On the first Sabbath about thirty or forty children were assembled of all ages and sizes, with wondering eyes; and in a few moments I found myself seated in a chair before six boys, whom I at once recognized as some of the worst village urchins, always to be seen at the "depôt," or on the "hotel steps," laden with baskets of apples and pea-nuts, their own best customers. I was about to ask for more hopeful subjects, but our earnest superintendent only held out to me the class-book and pencil—and I was alone with my destiny.

Among the names, I registered Andrew Jackson, Andrew Jackson, Jr., Marquis Lafayette, George Washington, and Byron Clarke. When about to inquire the cognomen of the last, I was forestalled by his calling out, in a stentorian voice, "My name a'n't nothing but *Bill Jones;* but I guess you have heard of the boy who sings nigger songs and dances Jim Crow at the 'Harrison House.'" He was unfortunately not mistaken in his notoriety, and the task before me assumed a new magnitude. None of them could read, and after half an hour of A B C, I proceeded to ask some simple questions of Bible history, of which I soon found that they knew absolutely nothing: their ideas of God, even, were as wild as those of the little Hindoos. So I began at the beginning. I spoke of the six days of creation; then of the deluge. When in my account of the ark and its wondrous freight, I was interrupted by one. "Did they have bears?" "Yes," I answered. "And lions?" "Yes." "Elephants?" "Yes." "Monkeys?" "Yes." And finally Billy Jones, all eagerness, "Did they have a *clown?*" And I found to my utter dismay that my youthful auditors, certainly not incapable of association of ideas, had conceived of Noah merely as the proprietor of a menagerie travelling in that wild waste of waters. Truly this was fallow ground. But our superintendent only smiled encouragement, and bade me go forward.

Sabbath after Sabbath rolled on, and rain or shine my six boys were always in their places. They had learned to love the school, especially the sweet hymns; and their quick sympathies had gone out to one who at least always tried to treat them gently and kindly. Of their affection I had many unmistakable proofs. Once I remember walking in one of the quiet streets. I was suddenly startled by three sonorous cheers, and looking up I saw the "Marquis," Andrew Jackson, and Byron Clarke. Though not precisely the most agreeable greeting for a young lady, I could not in my heart do less than wave a return. Again, they frequently brought to our door presents of flowers and fruit. In one instance the latter bore such a striking resemblance to some rosy-cheeked apples in a neighbor's orchard that I was forced to reprove the boy, and the next Sabbath took for our "lesson talk" the eighth commandment. Not many days after the same child made his appearance at the kitchen, his hands filled with the first pond-lilies of the season; and as he gave them to me he said, "There, Miss Esther, you will like them, for *they's honest; God growed them in the outlet.*" Never, from that day to this, have flowers brought more true gladness to my heart than did those pure white blossoms, plucked by swarthy hands in the "outlet" where "God growed them."

We established a missionary society among them, and many a penny, previously devoted to fire-crackers and the like, now found its way down the red chimney of our "savings bank." Poor Bill Jones had less to give than any of the boys, and this I plainly saw troubled him a great deal. He had stopped dancing "Jim Crow," first on Sabbath, and of late on week-days; and this being his chief source of revenue, his spare pennies were few and far between. One day, with a bright face, he asked me "if it was not right to do good on Sundays?" Of course I replied yes; and then "if it was wrong to take money for doing good on Sundays?" This was a nice distinction—one which I felt him not capable of understanding should I attempt it. So I simply said, "No, I thought not." Though feeling rather curious, I had no opportunity just then of asking as to these pious earnings. Next Sabbath the teachers were requested to remain a moment. A gentleman arose, not a member of our school, saying that a few hours since he had witnessed a scene which had so touched his heart that he could not forbear cheering us with the glad tidings. Passing the "Harrison House," he noticed that the invariable group of Sunday-noon loungers had deserted their post. Just then his ear was caught by a clear melodious voice singing. It seemed to come from the bar-room. Yes, as he drew near, from the open windows of that den of pollution floated out on the summer air the words:

"Watchman, tell us of the night,
What its signs of promise are."

He stepped upon the low platform and looked in. On a table sat a negro boy. About the room were hard-faced young men, and those older, on whose bloated features intemperance had set its livid brand. But they were all listening. The singer finished the last verse, and then began again. This time he sang, "Jesus, lover of my soul."

My own eyes were dimmed, said the gentleman, as he came to the lines,

> "Vile and full of sin I am;
> Thou art full of truth and grace."

It seemed as if for a moment an angel's wing brushed away the shadow from those darkened hearts, and tears moistened cheeks long unused to heart-rain. The singing stopped. "Go on, go on, we will pay you more," said one and another. "I cannot now," answered the boy; "it is time for Sunday-school, but I will sing again next Sunday, if you'll come." And as he put into his pocket the coppers that were handed him, he said, "I wouldn't take these, only I am going to send them to the heathen. I'll sing you the hymn —it's beautiful—about 'Greenland's icy mountains;'" and humming it to himself, "Bill Jones" left the bar-room.

Reader, should it ever be your good fortune to walk down this thickly-shaded village street on a Sabbath morn, you might within those very halls, now pure and white, hear the rich baritone voice of "Bill Jones" leading in some song of Zion, and with him many others, "plucked as brands from the burning."

XXIII.

THE CONVERSION AND CULTURE OF CHILDREN.

IMMEDIATE conversion ought to be the aim and expectation of every faithful Sabbath-school teacher. It is indeed a poor excuse to suffer a child to drown because we have but *one* opportunity of saving it. When a child is in danger of perishing, we do not first try to educate it, but to *save it*. The fact evidently is, that the great mass of children ought to be led directly to Christ and become child-Christians without delay; and multitudes would so become, methinks, if parents and teachers and pastors had sufficient confidence in the power of God's Word and Spirit, and had faith for the early conversion of children to God.

Nearly one and a third centuries ago that great divine, Jonathan Edwards, of Northampton, wrote the account of the conversion, as he thought, of little *Phebe Bartlett*, at the early age of four years, together with her Christian life for one year thereafter, and the evidences of a gracious change of her heart. The little book has been published since in many of the languages of Europe. Little Phebe Bartlett lived for sixty years after this, and neither herself nor her friends ever doubted that she truly met with a saving change of heart at the early age named by President Edwards. Many of our most learned divines and most devoted and useful Christian ladies date their conversion to the early age of three, four, five, and six years.

We have heard many pastors declare in Sabbath-School Conventions—two on one occasion—"That they never could remember when they did not love the Lord Jesus with all their heart;" and we believe with the pious Richard Baxter that if Christian parents were faithful in the use of the means God has put in their hands, the most of their children would be converted before they are old enough to understand a sermon.

It is a fact that should never be forgotten, that the children, even the little children of our Christian families and Sunday-schools, all *want* to be Christians more than they want anything else. Little ones of five or six years tell us that they wet their pillows night after night with tears of sorrow for sin, and they long for some one to lead them to Jesus, more than all earthly longings. Such is the testimony of devoted ministers and Christian ladies in great numbers, and many of us can realize it all, most bitterly, if we will only recall our early childhood and live that over again.

Said one little girl of four summers: "Mamma,

I should think that anybody that knows Jesus would *love him.*"

This is the feeling of properly-trained children in great numbers. They want pure, simple instructtion who Jesus Christ is, and what he is to *them.*

All the gospel knowledge really necessary for salvation lies, as it were, in a nutshell. The knowledge of their fall and sinfulness, and the atonement and redemption there is in Christ Jesus, and which, to a willing mind, can be taught in a few minutes, is all the knowledge really necessary for salvation. Really teach this and it will remain attached to the natural conscience for life, and only awaits the spark of grace from the Holy Spirit to descend and act upon it, and renew the heart and change the life.

This subject is one of overwhelming importance. It is the vital point of all Bible teaching. When Sabbath-school teachers learn the holy art of leading children to Jesus, then we may expect constant conversions. Sometimes we have known one-third of all the members of large Sabbath-schools to unite with the Church of Christ in a single season. Why should this not oftener be the case? Why should it not be the general rule in all our schools? and will it not be if the teachers will but have faith in God, faith in his Word, and faith in childhood, and *aim directly* to bring the children to Christ for salvation "at this time and under my instruction?" The great point is to get Bible truth, the Word of God, which is the sword of the Spirit, to bear directly on the conscience, heart and life of the child. Convince him thereby of his sin; then lead him by a simple trusting faith to Jesus' blood shed for *him*. Seek the proffered, willing aid of God's Holy Spirit believingly, and the work is done. "This is life eternal, to know thee, the only true God, and Jesus Christ whom thou hast sent."

Child-Culture.

Immediately connected with conversion is Christian child-culture and training in Bible knowledge, religious habits and service, and Christian character. Oh how important it is for child or man to have a kind, judicious sympathizing Christian friend at hand at every step, especially in the first year of life after conversion, to inquire and counsel as to difficulties and dangers! Secret and social prayer, the regular study of the Word, the social life and habits, the reading, the associations, the feelings, the imagination, the judgment, and the desire and tendencies all want watching, counselling, checking, guarding or instructing by one who is tender, candid, sincere and true. The whole life and usefulness much depends upon all this. The churches of Christ ought all to be such training-fields of Christian culture, but alas! we are sorry to confess that they are not generally so, and consequently largely fail in this their great work. To throw a little child, with only a spark of grace in the heart, into this world of wolves of temptation and error, with no one to watch over, counsel and guide, oh, it is sad indeed, and ought to excite the sympathy and prayers of all godly people. Let us associate and band Sunday-school workers together in earnest, in this great work of Christian culture and holy living—in little prayer-meetings teaching the children how to pray, how to resist temptation and fight against sin, and stand up for Jesus, how to overcome bad tempers and feelings, how to cultivate the disinterested missionary spirit of the gospel in caring for others, and doing good to others as we have opportunity. The children, like young trees from the nursery, need early "to be *planted* in courts of the Lord," if we would have them to grow up comely trees of righteousness.

Children's Prayer-Meetings.

Children, even little children, need to be taught *how* to pray. We all need to be taught to pray "as John also taught his disciples." This is especially true with children, because the prayers of the minister, or of the father around the family circle, are in most cases examples which a child will not try to follow. The words and expressions are, for the most part, quite unintelligible to a child, and consequently they must be taught in a different way. We must call the attention of a child to the particular things which he wants, or ought to thank God for, the particular sins which would be in his child's confession, and just the things he wants to ask God for in his own language every day and hour mingled with adoration and praise.

Children's prayer-meetings are well adapted to this. Some of our Sabbath-schools hold such a meeting at the close of each afternoon session. A gentleman who is just adapted to the work leads off the little boys who choose to attend, and a motherly lady goes with the girls into another room. We have known eighty to follow her into the room, and as many as half the number voluntarily follow her in prayers of two or three or four simple petitions for just what the little girls feel that they want. The meeting opens with singing a familiar hymn, and then a few appropriate verses and remarks, just adapted to kindle devotion in the little hearts, and then the little prayers follow freely and almost spontaneously. They soon learn to love to pray, and pray in real faith too, for the whole life of a little child is a life of faith. Of course it will all depend upon the manner in which these meetings are conducted, just as it is with any other meeting or religious service. In good hands they prove to be eminently successful and delightful. They teach the children how to pray, lead them into the habit of praying with the heart and voice, and with each other, and the influence on them, on their families, and the Sabbath-school is in every way most blessed.

Let the exercises of such meetings be short, natural and simple, with freedom and not constraint. A half or three-fourths of an hour is long enough, as they should not be prolonged. They ought to be universally adopted.

The Scholar.

It is a great privilege to become a faithful, punctual scholar in a well-ordered Sunday-school. Unnumbered blessings follow in the train. He should be enabled to appreciate this. It is a matter of primary importance that on his first introduction to the Sunday-school, he should be given distinctly to understand its true character, position, appropriate order and duties, and consent to a willing conformity to all.

Every scholar should be punctual, orderly, quiet, and respectful; he should learn and recite his lessons perfectly; never leave his seat without permission; address no one but his teacher, as a general rule; be obliging and pleasant to his class-mates, and set a good example of reverence for the holy Sabbath. In testimony of his appreciation of the benefits, and in some return for them, he will be diligent in bringing in new scholars, and also be particular to invite his parents and friends to the Monthly Concerts of Prayer for Sabbath-schools. The library book should be carefully read, so that a good account can be given of its contents to the teacher, if requested, and the special instruction of the teacher may, also, profitably become a subject for conversation with the parents. Above all, it is the duty and privilege of the scholar in the Sunday-school to learn the way, and find without delay, salvation by Christ in his own rich and joyous experience, and then to fill his heart and mind with a general and particular knowledge of Bible truths, and learn how to practice all in his daily life.

Nothing short of this experience should be the aim of every pupil.

XXIV.

PREACHING TO CHILDREN.

GREATER attention to the children in the public exercises of the Church is becoming a real necessity. With one-half of all the members of the families of the church and congregation before the pastor, as well as the population, under twenty years of age, and those in the most hopeful forming period of life, the question should forcibly arise, Are they not entitled to a far greater proportion of their pastor's labors and efforts than they have hitherto received? The General Assembly of the Presbyterian Church, at Dayton, Ohio, requested all their pastors to "give at least one-half of every Sabbath service to the children and youth." And Bishop Janes in a Methodist Episcopal Conference recently expressed the opinion that "the time is coming when there will be two sermons preached to children and youth where there is one to adults;" and Rev. Dr. McIlvaine, of Princeton, took very strong ground in favor of preaching to children in the New Jersey State Sabbath-School Convention at Elizabeth, two or three years ago. But we are met with this great difficulty at the outset: Many ministers say, "We cannot learn how to preach to children," to which we reply, confidently, "If you would only take one-quarter the pains to learn *how* to preach to children that you have to learn how to preach to adults, you would generally succeed to so great an extent as to astonish yourself and all your friends. Therefore, 1. The plan is practicable. 2. The subject is of overwhelming importance and imperative necessity. 3. Take a practical interest in the children. 4. Set about gathering and arranging materials for it. Have blank books to record every thought, fact, or illustration, and scrap books in which file in all good illustrations of Scripture truths from newspapers, magazines, etc. 5. Commence regularly and systematically to preach to children; for the way to learn how to preach to children is—*to preach to children*."

All this will involve the necessity of a watchful study of child-nature, child-language, and child-character. Something must be prepared especially adapted to attract and interest the children with fresh illustrations, etc. The Rev. Dr. Newton's sermons are admirable models. "The Peep of Day," "Line upon Line," and "Precept upon Precept," are fine specimens of pure child-language. Bible truths and illustrations are unequalled to interest children if they are only clearly presented, in a life-like, earnest manner, and broken up into little pieces for their use. It should ever be remembered that good preaching to children never fails to be most interesting to the older people. Good preaching to children by the pastor every week will greatly elevate all our monthly concert, missionary, and anniversary addresses, which should often be far more scriptural; and methinks, if the pastor would but preach one good scriptural sermon to the youth every Sabbath, both himself and his people would find a rich blessing in it.

Address to Children—In Outline.

The Child Jesus.

Luke ii. 40. "And the Child grew, and waxed strong in spirit, filled with wisdom; and the grace of God was upon him." *Grew* an infant, then a boy, afterward a man. Labored, suffered and *died* for you, for me.

I. See *The Child's Strength.* Not like Samson or David. Strong to do God's will, to do right. Resolute purpose, will, determination, etc. Jesus was strong to learn, to teach, to submit, to reprove and suffer. Strong to resist the world, flesh, and the devil. Strong for self-control.

II. See *The Child's Wealth.* Not Gold, Diamonds, etc., but *Wisdom.* How he got it? He gathered it. Where? *Bible*, doctors in temple, from the Spirit, from the world, etc.

III. See *The Child's Beauty.* The grace of God. Not beauty of face. Perhaps he had lost his beauty, "his face was so marred." It was beauty within; meek and quiet spirit; beauty of holiness, of obedience, of humility, of love.

1. God thought him beautitul. "In his Father's likeness," "All of his glory," etc.

2. Angels thought him beautiful. "They wondered and adored." "Angels desired to look."

3. Men thought him beautiful. "The Leper, the Demoniac, the Blind, the Palsied," etc.

Do you think him beautiful? or is there "no beauty in him that you should desire him?"

His strength he will give to you. "My strength is sufficient for thee."

His wealth he will give to you. "Filled with all the fulness of Christ."

His beauty he will put upon you. "No spot or blemish."

Oh! what think ye of Christ?

XXV.

CHILDREN'S MEETINGS AND MONTHLY CONCERTS.

HESE meetings are now becoming not only very important, but very interesting both to children and to adults. Sometimes Sabbath evening is set apart for it every week or every month; in other cases a week-day evening is chosen, and familiar and instructive lectures given. In other instances, again, a public children's meeting follows the regular teaching hour on Sabbath afternoons. If well conducted, these meetings are among the most acceptable and profitable and crowded of all the religious assemblages in a community.

The great word to study in the plan of such a meeting is—*adaptation.* It should be adapted not only to the little children, but also to the older ones, and especially to the young men and women, as well as parents and friends, who may be present. If it is held on the Sabbath, the great idea of worshipping God should never be lost sight of for a single moment. The reply may be—" To do this, and at the same time to adapt all the services to all the various ages and classes, is a very difficult matter." Of course it is difficult, but not impossible. The speaker to children, when in the presence of adults, should always choose a train of thought and illustration which will reach the children not only, but interest, instruct, and impress the older ones. A little special preparation and saving of materials just adapted to such occasions will accomplish it. The hymns and music should be appropriate and devotional, and only such as the children are familiar with and love to sing. The prayers should be short and simple, in order that all the children can join in them. A few verses only of Scripture should be read, but let them be made plain and interesting to all.

In some schools the Sabbath lesson is reviewed by the superintendent and illustrated, followed by five-minute remarks on the lesson by the teachers or friends present. In other places the children will bring scriptural texts to prove "what God says about obeying parents," about the holy Sabbath, about intemperance, or gambling, or lying, etc., interspersed with remarks. At other times a verse of Scripture, with the word "love" or "faith" or "heaven," etc., may be given by the scholars, improved, with instructive comments upon the passages, by the superintendent or pastor. At one concert we heard the children recite, by classes, the Scripture lessons of the last quarter, and the teachers recited the pastor's texts which he had preached from during the past three months. This was followed by an appropriate address, and all produced a most solemn effect. The history of a Scripture event, or character, or epoch will always furnish an abundance to interest. We do not favor elaborate or strained efforts. "Simple and Scriptural" would be our motto, and full of life, and the children and all will enjoy it exceedingly. Sometimes a report of the school incidentally, or the reading of a Christian letter or the words of a Christian visitor, may be timely. Let everything be prepared beforehand, and have no delay or hesitation.

XXVI.

AUXILIARY ASSOCIATIONS.

Youths' Temperance Societies.

HE terrible scourge of intemperance is making sad progress in our land. Whole families, men, women, and children, are desolated by it. Beer, domestic wines, cordials, and even medical prescriptions, are all made to contribute to, and swell this river of death. The only safe and sovereign remedy is—*total abstinence.* This conservative principle, in order to be the most effective, should be fully inculcated in early childhood; for our young men, after stimulating their appetites, often lose all power to stop. Therefore the children in our families and Sunday-schools ought to be early trained in abhorrence of all that leads to this dangerous and vicious course. Drinking leads to falsehood and deception, hypocrisy and dishonesty, impurity, and sometimes to murder. No love of parents or children, husband or wife, reputation, influence, character or wealth is sufficient to restrain.

It is therefore fitting that our youth be early instructed and guarded against the steps toward this great evil. Particularly ought the children in our Sabbath-schools to be made familiar with what God has said on this subject in the Bible. These texts should be often repeated by the scholars and explained and enforced by their teachers. Many fathers will say: "Rather let my son be an abject slave for life than to fall a victim to this degrading, destructive habit of intemperance." The question arises, When and how this can best be taught? We are always careful to protect Sabbath-schools from any diversion from the regular Scripture lesson of the day. The Bible and Bible-teaching is the glory of Sabbath-schools. Therefore we would never allow temperance or missionary work, or singing, or addresses to interrupt it. It is preferable in communities, we think, to take Saturday afternoons for a month or two for this purpose. Say, meet in the largest church at three to four and a half o'clock or three and a half to five o'clock P. M. Organize a Youths' Temperance Society. Appoint a discreet youth of fourteen or sixteen years President, with other officers, with a committee to arrange for each meeting. Secure good, fresh, appropriate speakers, and never allow a dull, heavy orator to occupy the children's attention. Instruction, life-like and adapted must constantly prevail. Some of the older boys, twelve to eighteen years old, may prepare and recite a ten-minute speech or appeal to their associates. The young ladies may write brief essays, giving their views upon the subject, which may be read. Secure as speakers the ministers, lawyers, etc., of the place, who can sustain attention, and who are known to be temperance men. Select and appoint twelve boys and the same number of girls, who shall circulate the pledge and obtain signatures. Continue the meetings only so many weeks as shall be needed and the interest shall be fully sustained, and then discontinue them for a few months. It will be necessary, however, to have some such temperance revival once in six to twelve months, in every place, to keep the cause in the ascendant and save the children, and the meeting and the result will be delightful to all. We have known a thousand pledges taken in this way, within a few weeks, in a country village of twenty-five hundred population.

In some schools the children recite in the monthly concert, texts which tell us what the word of God says about intemperance, and brief addresses are added. Another plan, which succeeds admirably in many Sabbath-schools, is to organize "Bands of Hope," on the plan which originated in Scotland in 1847, and in America in 1855. The pledges exclude not only other intoxicating liquors, but beer, cider, and also tobacco and profanity. They have a regular constitution, and forms of conducting them, with catechisms, hymns, dialogues, etc., all of which may be obtained at a trifling expense.

Their mode of admitting members is very impressive. The Temperance Catechism brings out a mass of facts on "The Origin and History of

Temperance Societies," "Nature of Intoxicating Drinks," "Fermentation and Distillation Process," "Brewing," "Alcohol and Mixtures," "Wines of Scripture," "Bible Abstinence," "Tobacco," "Profanity," etc.

Under the head of wine at the Lord's Supper, it holds that the Bible does not say what kind of wine was used, but we think it was unfermented, because at the time of the feast of the Passover the Jews were commanded to put away all leaven, and the word wine does not occur in any of the Evangelists when giving an account of the Lord's Supper. It was the fruit of the vine. Pliny, the Roman historian, has left an account of the various wines used at that time, in which he states that out of three hundred kinds of wine then in common use, only one would burn—that was called Falernian wine; that proves that two hundred and ninety-nine kinds of wine did not contain alcohol, and the chances, so to speak, are two hundred and ninety-nine to one in favor of Timothy's wine being unintoxicating. These extracts will suffice as specimens of what may be found in these little catechisms and tracts. They contain much valuable and needed information, whatever form of temperance effort is made on behalf of the children.

Juvenile Temperance Meetings are conducted, like any other good children's meetings, with much appropriate singing by the children, and prayer and reading of a few Scripture verses, and short, stirring, instructive addresses, so adapted that the interest must never for a moment flag. Sermons by the pastors are also amongst the most valuable ways of promoting sound temperance principles and practice.

Youths' Missionary Associations.

These are usually formed for a definite object—generally to support missionaries; to plant Sabbath-schools in destitute sections; or to aid in supplying poor schools with libraries. Every month they receive letters telling what has been done. They are organized by the appointment of a President, Secretary, Treasurer, and sometimes Collectors. A monthly missionary meeting is held and a yearly anniversary. At these meetings, besides reading the Scriptures, prayer, and singing by the children, reports are given of the doings and results, and letters are read giving details of the good accomplished. Addresses, brief and to the point, are then made by the pastor, superintendent, or one of the teachers, or by some invited friend of the cause. These missionary meetings should always be attended, not only by the pastor, teachers, and scholars, but also by the parents and members of the church and congregation, and should be made very interesting.

It has become quite popular now, in many schools, to organize each class into a distinct missionary circle, with a name and motto, as: "Earnest Workers," "The Harriet Newell Circle," "The

Lambs of Jesus," "The Buds of Promise," "Dew Drops," "Little Travellers," "Willing Hearts," "Modest Workers," "Cheerful Givers," "Young Timothies," "The Sowers," "The Guiding Stars," "Youthful Disciples," "Rose of Sharon," "Little Samuels," "The Reapers," "Olive Plants," etc. Each circle or class reports through a committee every month to the school. Sometimes each class has a small cheap banner, with its name printed on it.

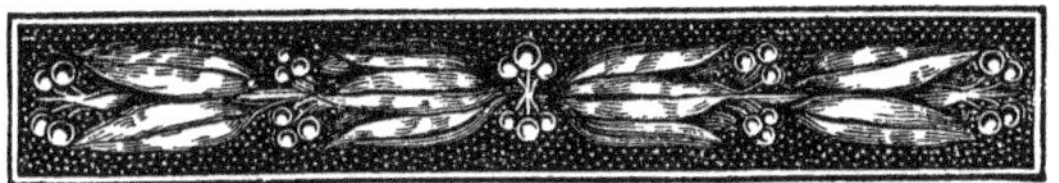

XXVII.

SABBATH-SCHOOL MUSIC.

HIS is a very important and attractive part of the exercises of a good Sunday-school, if rightly conducted. Good, pure, simple music, such as children love to sing, and words embodying the best Christian sentiments and feelings, should always be chosen. There is such an abundance of music at the present time, of an elevating, excellent character, that there is no excuse for adopting that which is doubtful. Some of the holiest Christian influences are carried weekly into little hearts and numerous families by these sweet songs of the children. It is well worth while for every Sunday-school to obtain a good supply of the best music, such as the children like; and they often love to meet on some afternoon or evening for the purpose of practising their music with their kind-hearted leader. It is the remark of a wise man: "Let me make the ballads of a nation, and I care not who makes its laws." How vastly important, then, it is to the future well-being of our youth that they be

well supplied with the choicest words and music to praise God in these little assemblies!

A few words of caution may be appropriate: Sing no more than that which will be truly worship and devotional on the Lord's day. Introduce all new hymns with great care to make the children *understand* the true sentiment before they sing it. Consequently, not more than one new hymn should be presented to the school on any one Sabbath. Let the practice in them take place on a week-day, or so as not to interrupt the worship of the Sabbath-school. Never should singing be introduced as an entertainment or diversion in the Sabbath-school, or made a hobby. Sacred music has a higher, holier mission. The hymns should be appropriate to the circumstances and occasion, and adapted in conformity to the Bible lesson of the day.

There is a great amount of music and hymns introduced into our schools of a very improper character. The hymns are nothing but a jingle of nonsense, and the music sometimes has very doubtful associations. All this should be avoided most carefully. Several of our Sunday-school music-book makers, it is said, have made a large profit out of the schools on the sale of a single book. We think this is not right. We are opposed to paying thirty-five cents for hymns and music in a book for children, when the music notes are of no use to the children, and the hymns can be sold for one-half of the price. Let the superintendent and music choristers have the books with the notes, of course. Besides, some of our best Sabbath-school superintendents are largely using Watts's and Wesley's and Cowper's hymns from our church hymn-books in their schools with great success, and they even sing church-music. If the hymns are adapted to the lesson, and are carefully explained to the children, so that they get a clear idea of their meaning, they sing them with great spirit and gladness of heart—such hymns as "When all thy mercies, O my God;" "On the cross uplifted high;" "Jesus, and shall it ever be;" "Hail my ever-blessed Jesus;" "My Saviour, my almighty Friend;" "There is a fountain filled with blood;" "Jesus, I my cross have taken," etc., etc. These, and many more like them, are used in preference to Sunday-school hymns, and the children greatly enjoy them. By the aid of stencil plates these hymns as needed, one for each Sabbath, are placed in large plain letters on sheets of white muslin, and suspended so as to be easily read by the whole school. Thus, every head is kept erect, and there is no diversion in looking over the hymn-book, and as a result the order is better, and the singing is better in every way.

XXVIII.

MEANS AND MEASURES.

Anniversaries.

ANNIVERSARIES have been quite common of late years; they seem to be very appropriate, and when well conducted, are productive of good. The summing up of the labors of the year in the annual report is often of more than local interest. The presence, orderly deportment, and singing of the children are all calculated to leave a happy, salutary impression. They are conducted with alternate hymns, prayers, addresses with the report, and are usually on the afternoon or evening of the Sabbath, with crowded audiences.

Here are brought out for prayer and review all the plans and work of the school for a twelve-month. The addresses should always be appropriate, instructive, and interesting to all, tending always to an increased spirituality and higher religious tone to the school. They should always reach the parents and friends present, as well as the children.

Excursions and Exhibitions.

Pic-nics, exhibitions, and the like, are all rather dangerous things in connection with Sunday-schools. In very sound, discreet, judicious Christian hands, they are often productive of good to all concerned; while under young, giddy, thoughtless management, they sometimes result in evil. Great caution should, therefore, be used. It will require much more grace and wisdom to conduct a Sunday-school exhibition than it will an ordinary service of the school. Says one writer: "Show-children are sometimes gotten up and exhibited, as if they were insensible to flattery as prize poultry." "A word to the wise is sufficient."

Premiums and Rewards.

We would carefully avoid entailing upon any Sunday-school a *system* of premiums and rewards, for several reasons. 1. It is needlessly expensive; 2. It is almost impossible to find a corps of teachers who are so good accountants as to be enabled to administer the system impartially; and thus jealousies and dissatisfactions arise both on the part of teacher and pupils; 3. Some of the very *kindest* teachers are often induced to reward those not *strictly* entitled to them, and as a consequence, loose and dishonest habits of business are taught the scholars; 4. After the novelty is worn off, the children learn to depend upon and claim their reward as a matter of right which they are justly entitled to, having earned it—

thus an improper habit and motive of action is entailed.

The pupils are debtors to the teachers, not the teachers to the pupils. We would not discourage the occasional judicious awarding of premiums to deserving scholars by the school, the teacher, or by benevolent individuals; only let them be given for a specific extra service—such as gathering new scholars, extraordinary punctuality, recitations, or sober attention for a long period of time; and let them be awarded so seldom as to be valued and influential.

Benevolent Contributions.

Benevolent contributions in our Sunday-schools are assuming an attitude of much importance, and it is, therefore, a point that needs to be well guarded from danger. It is very important that our children be early taught the principles and practice of benevolence; of caring for the ignorant and destitute, and doing them good according to their several abilities. They should especially be taught to *earn* and *save* money, instead of asking parents for it. Let it all be real and sincere. Great care should also be taken with the children to give for definite objects, and thus secure for them careful reports of what is done with their money. We should, however, most strictly conform to these legitimate objects, and on no account permit them to interfere in any way with the great work of teaching the Bible; and guard them especially against being so conducted as to foster pride, envy, and vain-glory. This can and should be done. The small penny rivulets of the millions of Sunday-school children, uniting, have swelled to a mighty stream, enlivening and refreshing many a dark, moral waste in our own and other lands, carrying untold blessings to myriads, and therefore, we are the more solicitous to keep the fountain pure and free.

Catechisms.

Most church and many mission schools adopt and successfully and regularly teach the great system of religious truths contained in these excellent compendiums of Christian doctrine. Sometimes one Sabbath a month, and sometimes a part of one, is allotted to this service, and not unfrequently the pastor meets with them, and reviews the lesson. It is preferable, however, to appoint a special service for the catechism, so as to let nothing interfere with the Scripture lesson of the day. "To the law and to the testimony."

There is a great want, however, of a sound, good catechism, translated into the best language of children of the present day, so that they can the more readily receive the truth into their understandings.

Two Sessions.

Most of the schools in the city of New York and vicinity, and some other cities, hold two sessions a day. The reasons they give for this course are, that teachers have not time faithfully to make the deep, permanent impression on the hearts of their pupils in one session that they think is necessary; that they cannot do justice to themselves, the children, or the lesson; that no thorough system of teaching can be carried out with one session; that the schools with one session, as a general rule, have only a struggling, lingering existence, and that neither pupils nor teachers will consent to return from two, to one session a day. With two sessions, they say, they have time to go over, *finish*, and *apply* the lesson, hear the enforcement or illustrations of the superintendent, and several times sing their sweet songs of Zion. Besides, they find their rest in the hearty service. Change from the Sabbath-school to a sermon is a relief, and change is rest. So that faithful, earnest teachers very rarely complain of too much labor or fatigue. Every church and school, however, determines this question for itself.

Constitution and By-Laws.

Sunday-schools usually adopt a few plain rules to govern them; we therefore give a simple form:

ART. 1. This Sabbath-school is connected with the —— Church, or shall be called the —— Sabbath-school.

ART. 2. It shall consist of a Superintendent, a Secretary, a Librarian, and as many teachers and scholars as may be duly received and appointed. The usual duties will be assigned to the different officers of the school.

ART. 3. This school shall open at —— o'clock in the morning, and —— o'clock in the afternoon, and each session shall continue one hour and ——.

ART. 4. On the first —— of January, or July ——, the terms for which all the officers are elected each year shall expire, and the teachers shall proceed by ballot, at such time, to elect new officers, or to re-elect the old ones.

ART. 5. Strict order shall be observed, and all the rules conformed to, by every one connected with the school, and no one shall leave the room until the close of the school, without permission.

ART. 6. The annual meeting, or anniversary, shall be held in the month of ———, at which time reports for the year shall be made, and an address by the pastor, or some other person who may be invited. Quarterly meetings for business, and weekly meetings for mutual assistance and counsel, and for the study of the lesson, shall be held by the teachers and officers.

ART. 7. This Constitution may be amended at any annual meeting, and By-Laws may be made or amended at any quarterly meeting, by a majority of all the teachers.

The By-Laws should define when and where teachers' meetings, missionary meetings, temperance or boys' meetings, or social Christian gatherings, may be held; and also what penalty, if any, for absence from teachers' meetings, etc.; also any other necessary objects may be included in the specifications of the By-Laws.

XXIX.

SABBATH-SCHOOL GUARDIANS.

Parents.

ARENTS are the divinely appointed guardians of their children. There is no shrinking from their responsibility except by unfaithfulness, and no evading it without guilt. In a few short, fleeting hours parents hold a position of honor and responsibility unparalleled in the duties of any human being.

In the case of Christian parents we believe that God has given them the power to paralyze the influence of the best Sabbath-school teacher or pastor in the land. If they give the cold shoulder to the Sabbath-school, they ought to understand that they will generally destroy its entire influence for good upon their children. Therefore they ought actively and heartily to co-operate with the Sabbath-school teacher and pastor in this work with the young. Parents who are not Christians cannot present so mighty a barrier; but every parent holds an important relation to the teachers and the school.

Parents should watch over the school, often visit

it, and manifest a deep interest in it. They should also notice and kindly check any tendency to error in doctrine or practice. They may counsel and suggest in every appropriate way whatever will advance its best interests, and they should personally know and kindly recognize the teacher as the friend of their children, and welcome and aid him in his visits to their homes. They should also contribute liberally and cheerfully to the support of the school, and particularly to the library. They should see that their children punctually attend school, commit their lessons to memory, and thus co-operate with the voluntary unpaid teacher, in giving their children the best and most valuable of all knowledge, and by God's blessing leading them to Christ for salvation.

Parents, accept the teachers to supplement and aid your efforts to save your offspring, but never, in any case, allow anything to supersede or lessen your obligations or spiritual labors for your own children.

Pastors.

We are fully convinced that our Sabbath-schools will never rise to what they ought to be until our pastors become the well-instructed leaders in this great work. We laymen are not in all cases sufficiently reliable nor fitted to be the leaders. We should take the place assigned to us by the Rev. Dr. Kirk, of Boston, in the State Sunday-School Convention of Massachusetts, when he said he "loved to recognize Sabbath-school teachers as lieutenants in the great army in which Christ Jesus has made him one of the captains."

Our Sabbath-schools, churches and ministers must all rise together. They should always keep closely together. It is here that Christians find a good working field under the training of the pastor, who is the pastor of the Sunday-school as well as of the church. It is here that the Church finds a great field of labor and her largest additions. Some pastors simply give their Sunday-schools their patronage and approbation. This is not sufficient. Much more is needed. Active co-operative service and direction are wanted. Sometimes pastors must needs act as superintendent of their own Sabbath-schools, and conduct their own teachers' meeting for a time, until they can train brethren and fit them to be superintendents. It is not lecturing, or preaching to, on the subject that we so much need as how to superintend, how to prepare the lesson, how to visit, what to teach, how to teach and lead to Christ, and how to conduct teachers' meetings.

The Sabbath-school enfolds the lambs of the flock. The pastor should, of course, watch over it very carefully and very tenderly. Every Sabbath he should at least walk through the school to encourage, by his presence, the weary teachers and scholars in their work of faith and labor of love. Many of the best pastors in our land make this an invariable rule. The teachers need their pastor's counsels and assistance in the school, the teachers' meetings and concerts of prayer, as well as in the pulpit. Here he will find his true working men and women, and if any of the church have especial claims upon him, they surely do have.

We need our pastors' presence and counsel in all our conventions and gatherings of teachers. They are *ex-officio* members of all. We also need their help in calling out the membership of the churches; in model sermons and model scriptural addresses, and teachings to children for instruction and for example. In fact, we feel that we must rely upon our ministers to raise up and make our Sunday-schools what they ought to be—the great training-schools of the Church, and the fitting field of labor for her large membership. As a matter of necessity, and as a matter of propriety, we throw ourselves as Sabbath-school workers upon the pastors, and call earnestly upon them for personal aid and comfort, in the strong assurance that our appeal will receive a warm and favorable response.

The Church.

The Church of Christ is the grand centre and radiating point of all our Christian efforts. The Sabbath-school is simply the Church of Christ *itself* putting forth its legitimate *action*. Says Dr. Baldwin: "It is the *workshop* of the Church for all working Christians." Here she trains her members for personal service and leads the lambs into the true fold. The nearer in sympathy our Sunday-schools are kept to the churches the better it will be for all; and if superintendents and teachers wish to give their labors a permanently successful character, they cannot make too short work in leading their pupils to the Church of Christ; at first, perhaps, as only attending, hearing members, then believing, obeying members. The outer, or mission-schools, are stepping-stones to churches. If mission-churches are established with those schools, as is often the case, the Church will be on convenient ground. Sunday-schools, Bible, and tract mission efforts should be superintended and sustained by the churches. Especially should the churches stand by the Sunday-schools—the nurseries of the Church—and see that they want no good thing. Rooms, seats, books, and all appliances, should be freely provided for the school; for the future hopes of Zion are there. By far the greater number of her additions from the world come through the Sabbath-school.

Not one-half of the children of our land, or scarcely of any State in our land, can be found on the Lord's day in any of our Sabbath-schools.

The churches ought, without delay, to supply this lack. Surely we can ask no less of them. The churches are abundantly able to do this. They have never trained and sent forth as Sabbath-school teachers as many as fifteen per cent. of their great membership, and not half the children are yet taught. Let the churches train and send forth thirty per cent. of their members, and the neglected are all reached and the work is done. Therefore the question is one of disposition, will—not ability.

The Community.

The community has a deep personal interest in the Sunday-school, and has corresponding duties. Thousands of youth are every year saved from prison and from crime by this institution. The three hundred and fifty or four hundred thousand voluntary Sunday-school teachers of our land comprise a moral police, to which the community are immensely indebted, whether they are sensible of it or not. It recently cost New York city more than twenty-five thousand dollars to convict one murderer, who had been neglected from a child. That sum of money would have paid his board for sixty years, or sustained twenty thousand children in mission-schools for a whole year. The Sabbath-school is a cheap and simple agency to give the gospel to the millions. It is the cheapest civilizer extant.

Thousands of the best patriots, statesmen, and Christians of our own and other lands love to acknowledge their immense obligations to the Sabbath-school, for what they are, and what they hope to be. Said the Bishop of London: "The Sunday-school has *saved* the manufacturing districts." And the Earl of Shaftesbury declared: "To you, Sunday-school teachers, is entrusted the future of the British empire."

Many thousands of parents in our land, who are entirely neglecting the religious instruction of their children, can bring them to the Sabbath-schools, where four hundred thousand voluntary teachers stand cheerfully ready to teach them, without money and without price. Like the waters of the river of life, this stream runs free. Let parents see to it that their children are regularly there. The community should do all they can to help forward this beneficent voluntary scheme of public education, acknowledge their real obligation to the teachers, offer them rooms in their public school buildings, and by the pressure of a sound public sentiment, increase the uniform attendance, particularly from the ignorant and neglected classes.

XXX.

MISSIONARY AGENCIES.

Neighborhood Prayer Meetings.

HE Sabbath-school teacher in his work finds it convenient to do incidentally a vast amount of good. He distributes copies of the Bible and Testament, tracts and good reading, helps the needy to a place for work, relief, etc., etc. Among other means the opening of neighborhood prayer-meetings has been greatly blessed. A score or two of friends and neighbors meet on a week-day evening in a tenant-room or house convenient, and there two or three of the Sabbath-school teachers conduct a familiar religious service, which, if appropriate and interesting, often results in conversions and bringing individuals into Christian associations and influences, and sometimes leads to the reformation of a whole neighborhood. Our young women teachers sometimes conduct these meetings with great success and profit.

A good mission-school of teachers has sometimes sustained a dozen weekly neighborhood prayer-meetings. All these plans are equally adapted to cities or country villages.

Bible Readers.

Of late years the employment of pious and discreet women as Bible readers has accomplished the most blessed results. These constant visitors penetrate many a dark alley and cellar, and rescue from intemperance, starvation, destitution and crime those who would not otherwise be reached. They also comfort, and instruct, and aid multitudes of poor ignorant mothers who really know not what to do, and sustain many neighborhood prayer-meetings and mothers' meetings. Sometimes they are supported by the Bible Society, and in other cases by the City Mission, but oftener by the mission or church Sabbath-schools and churches.

Young women who are adapted to the work leave their sewing and other labor, and receive a salary sufficient for their support in this service. Some of the poor ignorant, reclaimed women make, when trained for it, most excellent Bible readers.

Industrial Schools.

Industrial schools are usually for girls from the streets, who are picked up, washed, supplied with a dinner, taught to read, to sew, and other useful employments; besides, good manners and good dispositions are carefully cultivated. They are also taught to sing our choicest Sabbath-school hymns, and receive much valuable counsel and sound Christian instruction from their kind teachers and friends. These schools are doing a most excellent work. They are held every day in institutions. In Sunday-schools they are generally held only on Saturday afternoons, and a score of ladies volunteer to come and teach them. In either form they are very useful.

Boys' Meetings.

This is a modern thing, but it grew out of the warm, earnest sympathy of excellent Christians for the worst class of street-boys of New York. They were attracted by the fine music taught them, the interest and kindness manifested toward them, and the stirring, pointed, interesting stories in which religious truth was clothed as it was spoken to them; and the energy and capability which first started those meetings could sustain them now on the same basis. Latterly, they assume more the general form of young people's meetings, being composed of a majority of boys and girls from Christian families, or at least Sunday-schools, and most of them contain but a few of the rough street-boys. They are a stepping-stone to a good Sunday-school. Youths' attractive papers are circulated at the close. Interesting popular lectures, made very familiar and plain, on practical subjects, are sometimes enjoyed on the week-day evenings.

XXXI.

THE QUESTION BOX.

AMONG the modern improvements in our Sabbath-school meetings the "Question Box," or "Drawer," is worthy of particular mention. Slips of paper are placed in the hands of the members of the Convention or Institute, who are requested to write upon them any question which may be suggested to their minds, and on which they would like to gain the opinions of others. These questions are, from time to time, dropped into a box provided, and left at the door or on the platform. Otherwise, they are collected by a committee and handed up to the conductor, who, at the proper time, either answers them himself or designates some other person or persons to answer them. In this way a vast amount of clear and correct information is often gained, and that of a kind exactly adapted to present wants. No exercise in an Institute is more directly profitable than the question box often proves to be.

It of course depends entirely upon the correct knowledge and grasp of the persons who essay to answer; for either truth or error are alike rapidly propagated in this way. Therefore the greatest care should be taken that no one be allowed to answer questions in this way, who cannot, as the result of mature and deliberate observation or experience, comprehensively look on all sides of the question, and be careful to do justice to all its points. No "snap" judgment should be taken, no witticism indulged in, and no dogmatic answers allowed. On the contrary, the utmost fairness and candor is indispensable.

For illustration of this subject, the following examples of questions and answers will suffice:

1. How can we obtain good teachers? *Answer.* Train them up in your Bible-classes and teachers' meetings. Be on the lookout for suitable persons and excite their interest by conversations on the value, the details, and working of the Sabbath-school.

2. Would you recommend the grading of Sabbath-schools? *Answer.* We like the word *adaptation* better, for there must be *that* in all good teaching; there must be, also, advancement and thorough Bible instruction. But we fear that an attempt to grade Sunday-schools would stiffen and injure them, for we have but one hour in a week, while the public schools have six hours per day and five days in a week, with a dozen grades of text-books, and paid, disciplined teachers. Besides, we have never found a successful Sabbath-school with more than the three

regular gradations; viz., the infant-classes, the intermediate classes, and the young men and women's classes.

3. Would you ever employ unconverted teachers? *Answer.* Get the *best* teachers you can; the most pious, the best skilled and regular. When you have taken the *best* you can get, you have done all your duty, and God does not require any more, for he accepts according to what we have. In some remote sections it is simply a question between accepting moral and upright young people or no teachers. They can teach the elemental truths of religion, and God has repeatedly employed the most unworthy persons to deliver his most solemn messages. Therefore get the *best* teachers you can. It is the message, not the messenger.

4. Do you approve of one uniform lesson for the whole school? *Answer.* Yes, by all means; and then concentrate all the exercises, the prayers, the hymns, the addresses, as well as all the teaching, directly upon that one portion, so that it will be impressed upon all, as it was upon a little boy who walked up to the blackboard and pointed to the drawing of an altar and the bleeding lamb upon it, saying, "It was *that* all day, wasn't it, Jimmy?" Let the infant-class have the central verse for their lesson.

5. Would you expel a bad boy? *Answer.* I never did, and never would do so, except as a last resort, after trying every available resource.

6. How can we get the parents, pastors, etc., interested in the Sabbath-school? *Answer.* Go to them and respectfully ask their counsel and advice about the Sabbath-school. Get them to investigate and inquire, give them hints and information, and thus excite their interest.

7. Is it consistent for a Sabbath-school teacher to play at cards, dance, etc.? *Answer.* Cards are gamblers' tools, and we should beware of them. Besides, the teacher's time is too precious. I have never danced since I first became a Sabbath teacher, nearly forty years ago. It will lessen Christian influence. "If meat make my brother to offend," says Paul, "I will eat no flesh while the world standeth."

8. What is the best way to get rid of inefficient teachers? *Answer.* Treat them with the most tender consideration. Call upon them and give them some hints about a verse in the lesson, which they can use with this or that scholar in their class. I have always found it better to make poor teachers over, than to look up and train new ones.

9. How can you restore order in a disorderly class? *Answer.* The teacher must first be in the most perfect order and control himself, and he will soon control the class, if his patience holds out.

10. What is the pastor's position in the Sabbath-school? *Answer.* He is the pastor of the lambs in the Sabbath-school as well as of the church.

11. Is it best to reprove scholars or teachers in presence of the class or classes? *Answer.* NEVER

12. Who are to elect the superintendent? *Answer.* In most cases he should be elected by the teachers, not by the scholars.

13. Who appoints the teachers? *Answer.* They are generally appointed by the superintendent.

14. How long ought a lesson to be? *Answer.* Six to ten verses, and forty minutes' time for the teacher.

15. What is the best way of training teachers? *Answer.* Get for them *The Sunday-School Times*, and attract them into the regular weekly teachers' meeting.

16. How shall we retain young men and women? *Answer.* Get a teacher who loves, honors, and respects them and can understand young people, and does not forget that he was once young. Then elevate the Sabbath-school, so that the young people will not be belittled in attending it.

17. Is there not danger that the Sabbath-school will induce a disrelish for the preaching service? *Answer.* We must certainly guard against such a result. The Sabbath-school must cling close to the Church of God.

18. How much money should be expended annually on a large mission-school? *Answer.* A fair Christian economy is *best.* I know of mission-schools, of four hundred scholars, sustained at an expense of less than four hundred dollars, including rent, that are better every way, they are more regular and successful, than some similar schools which expend

from one thousand to twelve hundred dollars per year.

19. How many children are there in all our Sabbath-schools? *Answer.* If the question refers to the United States, I think we may safely say that now we have, in Sabbath-schools, about four million children and youth, with about four hundred thousand teachers. A quarter of a century ago or so, the numbers were estimated at two million five hundred thousand, but this was when the great Western States were in their comparative infancy. The number rapidly increased to three millions, and then to three million five hundred thousand, and now our returns and estimates reach four millions. Great Britain has about the same number, both of teachers and scholars; but we do not think all other countries can raise the full number of Sabbath-school children quite up to *ten millions*, or the number of Sabbath-school teachers to a grand army of *one million* strong. The census of 1860 gave the number of persons in the United States, between the ages of five and sixteen, at nine millions (or only a few thousands less). As a consequence, we have the great aggregate of *five millions!* of unreached and uncared-for children and youth in our land. What an immense and hopeful missionary field here lies open at our doors! There is scarcely a State in our whole Union or a city which can truly report *one-half* of her children in any kind of a Sabbath-school on any given day. And yet some of our great

States are working very energetically and systematically. Witness the State of Illinois, which has organized every one of its one hundred and two counties during the past two or three years, by the voluntary and Sunday-school missionary labors of its Sunday-School Association, aided by other agencies. What this State has done, other States, if they will, can do, and the immense work before us, when systematically undertaken, is by no means a hopeless task.

The Answer Box.

Nearly allied to the question box is the answer box. It consists in this: At an appropriate time in an Institute, the conductor writes an important question on the blackboard—blank papers are distributed and all the members are requested to write their answers. For instance, all are requested to write upon the question, What is the great want of our Sabbath-schools? One writes, "The Holy Spirit, praying teachers, aim at conversions," etc. Another writes, "Good superintendents, devoted pastors and parents." Another writes, "Clear teaching, good order, and devout singing." Others, "The Bible needs to be exalted and applied;" "Make the Bible attractive to the children;" "Living, earnest teachers who love the children;" "Aim at salvation and Christian training." Or if the question should be, "How to prepare a Bible lesson?" one answers "1. Pray. 2. Read it over carefully. 3. Think and pray. 4. Look up the parallel passages. 5. Examine Commentaries, Dictionaries, etc. 6. Search out illustrations for each pupil. 7. How to apply truth to each and all." Another writes: "1. Fix on the subject early in the week, keep it constantly before the mind, trying to find illustrations anywhere and everywhere. 2. Endeavor to make it simple, yet interesting and practical. 3. Constantly seek divine direction."

At the close of a recess of ten minutes for writing and receiving the answers, they are taken up and read by the conductor, and then referred to a committee of three to digest and report upon at a future meeting. We get at the heart of the people in this way.

XXXII.

MISTAKES OF TEACHERS.

IT is a mistake to suppose that mere *talk* is teaching.

It is a mistake to think that hearing a Bible lesson recited, or the reading of questions from a book, or telling stories, is good Sabbath-school teaching.

It is a mistake to think that one who in manner and temper is impatient, dogmatic, overbearing, slow, heavy or dull, can be a good Sabbath-school teacher.

It is a mistake to suppose that one who is not understood, or is misunderstood, is a good teacher.

It is a mistake to suppose he who gossips with his class is a good teacher.

It is a mistake to suppose, because we have a general idea beforehand, that we shall be able to supply the details and illustrations as we go along.

It is a great mistake to underrate oral teaching, and overrate merely reading and reciting from the Bible.

It is a great mistake to think that our scholars are too young to appreciate a well-prepared lesson or a well-governed school.

It is a mistake of teachers to expect attention from motives of duty, or the sacredness of the day or importance of subject—nothing but real interest will secure it.

It is a mistake to teach as if all young children had the same *tastes*.

It is a great mistake to fail to arouse curiosity and awaken interest.

It is a mistake to suppose that we shall be understood without careful simplicity of language.

It is a mistake not to recall by questions the last Sabbath's lesson, and to treat lessons as if they were isolated; by all means connect them.

It is a great mistake for teachers to think that giving good advice or exhortation to children is as good as "breaking down" Bible truths with questions and answers.

It is a mistake to suppose that many common terms, such as "Providence," "grace," repentance, justification, etc., convey any meaning to children, ordinarily.

It is a mistake to attempt to purchase affection or attention by frequent gifts to children; neither by threats nor punishments.

It is a great mistake of Sabbath-school teachers to suppose that their work is that of a mere philanthropist—or a moral educator, or a mere promoter of social good order, or raising up of good citizens and children.

It is a mistake of teachers to expect a cold reception from parents.

It is a mistake of teachers to suppose that their manner and habits are unobserved by the children.

It is a mistake to avoid repetition with children—simplify and repeat.

It is a mistake to teach our children, that if they will be good and read the Bible, pray and join the Church, they will thereby go to heaven. Nothing but repentance toward God and faith in the Lord Jesus Christ will secure that.

It is a great mistake for Sabbath-school teachers ever to teach Bible truth without being really in *earnest*—calmly, cheerfully, seriously in *earnest.*

XXXIII.

HELPS FOR TEACHERS.

VERY thorough workman ought to have the best of tools to work with, and the teacher should be furnished with all needful helps. The *indispensable* books for a Sabbath-school teacher are—1st. A complete reference Bible—your own Bible. 2d. A Concordance. 3d. A good Bible Dictionary. Add to these, accurate and careful observation to see in the opening flower, the falling leaf, the events of the day and the providence of God, rich and apt lessons for youthful hearts. On opening my library door I notice upon the shelves most of the following books, which, with others that are now out of print, have accumulated to meet my real wants as a Sabbath-school worker, and none of which I would be willing to part with:

Bibles.

Family Bible, with Notes and Instructions.
Annotated Paragraph Bible, 2 vols.
Reference Bible, with Index and Maps.

Dictionaries, Cyclopædias and Commentaries.

Dictionary of the Bible. 1 or 3 vols.—*Smith.*
Dictionary of the Holy Bible.—*Robinson.*
Biblical Cyclopædia. 3 vols.—*Kitto.*
Cyclopædia of Biblical, Theological and Ecclesiastical Literature.—*McClintock and Strong.*
Encyclopædia of Religious Knowledge.—*Brown.*
Daily Bible Illustrations. 8 vols.—*Kitto.*
Comprehensive Commentary. 6 vols.—*Jenks.*
Critical, Doctrinal and Homiletical Commentary.—*Lange.*

Expository Thoughts on the Gospels.—*Ryle.*
Studies in the Gospels.—*Trench.*
Notes on the New Testament. 11 vols.—*Barnes.*
The Gospel Treasury.—*Mimpriss.*
A Year with St. Paul.—*Knox.*
The Parables.—*Guthrie.*
Notes on the Miracles.—*Trench.*
Introduction to the Study of the Holy Scriptures.—*Horne.*
Notes on the Old Testament. 5 vols.—*Barnes.*
Notes on the Bible. 8 vols.—*Bush.*

Books of Reference.

Complete Concordance.—*Cruden.*
The Bible Hand-Book.—*Angus.*
The Treasury of Bible Knowledge.—*Ayre.*
Bible Months.—*Groser.*
Introduction to the Study of the Scriptures.—*Nicholls.*
Biblical Antiquities.—*Nevin.*
Scripture Text-Book and Treasury.
English Synonyms.—*Crabbe.*
Works of Flavius Josephus.
The Steps of Jesus.—*Mimpriss.*
A Theological Dictionary.—*Buck.*

Bible Geography and Travel.

Historical Text-Book and Atlas.—*Coleman.*
Biblical Researches in Palestine. 3 vols.—*Robinson.*
The Land and the Book. 2 vols.—*Thomson.*
Geography of Palestine.—*Groser.*
Life-Scenes from the Four Gospels.—*Jones.*
Little Foot-Prints in Bible Lands.—*Vincent.*
Bible Atlas and Gazetteer.

Hand-Books of Instruction.

The American Sunday-School and its Adjuncts.—*Alexander.*
Forty Years' Experience in Sunday-Schools.—*Tyng.*
Thoughts on Sabbath-Schools.—*Hart.*
The Good Teacher.—*Henderson.*
The Sabbath-School.—*Inglis.*
The Christian Teacher in Sunday-Schools.—*Steel.*
Rise and Progress of Sunday-Schools.—*Power.*
The Teacher Taught.—*Packard.*
The Sabbath-School Teacher.—*Todd.*
Our Sunday-School.—*Abbot.*
Sunday-School Photographs.—*Taylor.*

The Teacher Teaching.—*Packard.*
Nature's Normal School.—*Gall.*
The Infant-Class.—*Reed.*
The Young Men's Class.—*Blacket.*
End and Essence of Sabbath-School Teaching.—*Gall.*
The Sabbath-School Concert.—*Trumbull.*
Hours with the Youngest. 2 vols.—*Gill.*
Helpful Hints for the Sunday-School Teacher.—*Vincent.*
Our Work.—*Groser.*
Teacher's Model and Model Teacher.—*Groser.*
The Use of Illustration.—*Freeman.*
Art of Questioning.—*Fitch.*
Illustrative Teaching.—*Groser.*
Model Sabbath-School Lesson.—*Wells.*
Art of Attention.—*Fitch.*
Introductory Class.—*Groser.*
Diamonds in the Dust.—*Reed.*
On Memory.—*Fitch.*
Training-Classes.—*Groser.*
Sunday-School Teaching.—*Whately.*
Teacher's Keys.—*Reed.*
Pictorial Teaching.—*Hartley.*
Bible Training.—*Stow.*
How to Teach.—*Groser.*
Senior Classes.—*Watson.*
Early and Infant-School Education—*Currie.*
The Child and the Man.—*Greenwood.*
Our Material.—*Groser.*
Sabbaths with My Class.—*Green.*

Anecdote and Illustration.

The Biblical Treasury.
Illustrative Gatherings. 2 vols.—*Bowes.*
Pilgrim's Progress.—*Bunyan.*
The Power of Illustration.—*Dowling.*
Illustrations of the Commandments.—*Cross.*
The Young Christian.—*Abbott.*
Anecdotes on the Old and New Testaments.
Moral Lessons.—*Cowdery.*
Bible Blessings.—*Newton.*
Bible Jewels.—*Newton.*
Lectures to Children. 2 vols.—*Todd.*
Great Pilot.—*Newton.*
Grapes from the Great Vine.—*Breed.*

Safe Compass.—*Newton.*
Truth made Simple.—*Todd.*
Rills from the Fountain of Life.—*Newton.*
Addresses to Children.—*Green.*
The Child's Bible Stories. 4 vols.—*Kelly.*
Children and Jesus.—*Hammond.*
Peep of Day.
Line upon Line.
Precept upon Precept.
Little Crowns, and How to Win Them.—*Collier.*

General Education.

Theory and Practice of Teaching.—*Page.*
Methods of Instruction.—*Wickersham.*
Outlines of Object-Teaching.—*Hailman.*
The Student's Manual.—*Todd.*
Home Education.—*Isaac Taylor.*
Primary Object Lessons.—*Calkins.*
The Elements of Moral Science.—*Wayland.*
The Observing Faculties.—*Burton.*
The Teacher.—*Abbott.*

Periodicals for Teachers.

The Sunday-School Times.—Weekly.—*Philadelphia.*
The Sunday-School Teacher.—Monthly.—*Chicago.*
The Sunday-School Teachers' Journal.—Monthly.—*New York.*
The Sunday-School World.—Monthly.—*Philadelphia.*
The Sunday Teachers' Treasury.—Monthly.—*London.*
The Sunday-School Teacher.—Monthly.—*London.*
Scottish Teachers' Magazine.—Monthly.—*Edinburgh.*

Periodicals for Youth.

The Wellspring.—Weekly.—*Boston.*
The Youth's Evangelist.—Semi-Monthly.—*Philadelphia.*
Sunday-School Advocate.—Semi-Monthly.—*New York.*
The Sabbath-School Visitor.—Semi-Monthly.—*Philadelphia.*
The Child's World.—Semi-Monthly.—*Philadelphia.*
The Young Reaper.—Semi-Monthly.—*Philadelphia.*
The Child's Paper.—Monthly.—*New York.*
The Child at Home.—Monthly.—*Boston.*
The Children's Hour.—Monthly.—*Philadelphia.*
The Carrier Dove.—Monthly.—*New York.*
The Child's Treasury.—Monthly.—*Philadelphia.*
The Youth's Temperance Banner.—Monthly.—*New York.*
Kind Words.—Monthly.—*Greenville, South Carolina.*

The Teacher's Covenant.

Impressed with the serious nature of the charge, will the faithful Sabbath-school teacher enter into a *written* engagement with his Saviour, in words somewhat like the following?—

1. *I promise* to be in my place punctually every Sabbath, at the time appointed, unless prevented by sickness, or some other cause so urgent that it would in like manner keep me from important worldly business.

2. *I promise*, in every such case of unnecessary absence, that I will use my utmost diligence to secure a suitable substitute, whom I will instruct in the character of the class and the nature of the duties to be performed.

3. *I promise* to study carefully beforehand the lesson to be recited by the scholars, and to have the subject in my mind during the week, so that I shall be likely to lay hold of, and lay up for use, anything that I may meet with in my reading or experience that will illustrate or enforce the lesson of the approaching Sabbath.

4. *I promise* to be diligent in informing myself about the books in the library, so that I can guide my scholars in selecting such books as will interest and profit them; also in becoming acquainted with other good books and tracts, so that I can always be prepared, as opportunities may occur, to lead their minds into right channels of thought.

5. *I promise*, whenever a scholar is absent from the class on the Sabbath, that I will visit that scholar before the next Sabbath, unless prevented by sickness, or by some other hindrance so grave that it would, under like circumstances, keep me from attending to important worldly interests.

6. *I promise* to visit statedly *all* my scholars, that I may become acquainted with their families, their occupations, and modes of living and thinking, their temptations, their

difficulties, and the various means of reaching their hearts and consciences.

7. *I promise*, if any of my scholars or their parents do not attend statedly any place of worship, that I will make the case known to the superintendent and pastor, and that I will use continued efforts to induce such children and their parents to go to church regularly.

8. *I promise* that every day, in my hour of secret prayer, I will pray distinctly, by name, for each one of my scholars, for their conversion, if they are still out of Christ; for their sanctification and growth in grace, if they are already converted.

9. *I promise* that I will seek an early opportunity of praying with each scholar privately, either at his house or mine, or in some other convenient place that may be found, and of asking him in a serious and affectionate manner to become a Christian.

10. *I promise*, when I have thus prayed and conversed with each scholar once, that I will begin and go through the class again, not omitting any, and not discontinuing my attempts, but going on faithfully, week by week, month by month, and year by year.

Signed,

______________________________.

THE END.

www.ingramcontent.com/pod-product-compliance
Lightning Source LLC
La Vergne TN
LVHW010252110826
845151LV00004B/1450
9781425522339